Boom or Bust

Boom or Bust

*Understanding and Profiting from a
Changing Consumer Economy*

By Douglas C. Robinson and Charles L. Sizemore, CFA

Matthew
Mowll-Wilson

iUniverse, Inc.
New York   Bloomington

Boom or Bust
Understanding and Profiting from a Changing Consumer Economy

iUniverse books may be ordered through booksellers or by contacting:

iUniverse
1663 Liberty Drive
Bloomington, IN 47403
www.iuniverse.com
1-800-Authors (1-800-288-4677)

Because of the dynamic nature of the Internet, any Web addresses or links contained in this book may have changed since publication and may no longer be valid. The views expressed in this work are solely those of the author and do not necessarily reflect the views of the publisher, and the publisher hereby disclaims any responsibility for them.

ISBN: 978-0-595-51003-0 (sc)
ISBN: 978-0-595-50365-0 (dj)
ISBN: 978-0-595-61729-6 (ebook)

Printed in the United States of America

iUniverse rev. date: 4/3/2009

Table of Contents

Acknowledgments

Special thanks to all those who aided us in preparing the content of this book. We would like to thank Harry S. Dent, Jr., Founder and CEO of HS Dent; Rodney Johnson, President of HS Dent; Harry Cornelius; and all of the members of the HS Dent Advisors Network for their insights and encouragement in writing this book.

We would like to acknowledge Scott Mitnick for sacrificing hours of his Hawaiian vacation to read, re-read, edit, and analyze our work. We received Scott's copy of the manuscript fresh from the beach, with the corners slightly curled from the moist sea air and with traces of sand in the margins. Scott was ruthless with the editing pen, and we now have a much better book as a result. Thanks for your hard work, Scott. Your critique was very much appreciated.

Rick Allen, President and CEO of Genesis Employee Benefits, Inc. deserves credit for teaching us virtually everything we know about retiree health obligations and how to mitigate them. Thanks for the education, Rick. And finally, special thanks to Lisa Lehtinen, Southwest Regional Vice President of Genesis Employee Benefits, Inc., for giving our manuscript a thorough review and making those last-minute recommendations that make all the difference. This book would not have been possible without the generous gifts of time and attention by all.

Introduction

Every day we are hit with a barrage of information, and much of it is related to the state of the economy. An informational overload, our morning newspapers, cable TV channels, and favorite web sites bubble over with stock quotes, advice from financial experts, commentary on Federal Reserve policies, and the occasional dire warning of impending "doom and gloom." With so much information and so many conflicting opinions, many people throw up their hands in despair and simply give up the hope of ever understanding it all. Some latch on to one expert's opinion, the guru of the day, and attach an almost mystical significance to his or her thoughts, ignoring all contrary evidence. Others look for a political explanation for every bend and twist in the economy, attributing prosperity to the party of their choice and blaming all hardship on the other party.

The sheer multitude of opinions guarantees that at any given time most of them will be wrong. Of course, some are never "wrong" because they never give a clear forecast to begin with. President Harry Truman famously asked for a one-handed economist because his advisers had a habit of equivocating with "on the one hand...but on the other hand...." One might compare an economist to an octopus given the number of "hands" they often list in their prognostications.

Most mainstream economic literature is of limited value for planning your life and your investments. It does not matter much in your retirement planning if GDP grew at exactly 4.1% last quarter vs. the consensus opinion of 4.2%. This is unlikely to impact major life decisions, such as whether to buy that new house of your dreams or whether you should send your child to that expensive private school. Monthly economic news releases are generally little more than statistical noise, far from deserving the sense of urgency they inspire among the news anchors on CNBC.

At the same time, many long-term facts and figures have little use for real planning as well. It is very small consolation to you that the stock market goes up 7% per year over the "long run" if you have just lost 50% in a major bear market, like that of 2008. This becomes even more true if you are in or near retirement. Sure, over time your portfolio *should* recover its losses. But as the economist John Maynard Keynes famously said, "in the long run, we're all dead."

In order to make real decisions, we need better information. And luckily, the information exists right at our fingertips. We will never be able to predict every twist and turn in the economy or in the financial markets. There is simply too much randomness in the short-term and too much dependence on human emotion. But just as people make the economy and markets random and erratic over short periods, they also tend to make it surprisingly predictable over the medium to long-term. In an economy that is 70% consumer spending, it is ordinary people that drive the economy, and, on average, people are very predictable. By understanding consumer behavior, it is possible to forecast the direction of the economy and even the multi-year direction of the stock market. Using demographic data, you can make critical forecasts for individual industries and real estate markets. Such data can also be used by governments (or would-be taxpayers) for everything from school construction to public pension systems.

In this book, we will attempt to break economics down to its core. What really matters? And how do we use this information to make better decisions? The pages of this book are full of valuable material, but it is not designed to simply give you the "answers." Instead, this book is designed to act as an instruction manual of sorts. Our goal is to help you ask the right questions.

We cover a lot of details in this book, and in an attempt to make it easier to digest we have divided it into sections:

- Part I of the book is a general discussion of the economic trends that will be affecting every American over the next several decades. Inspired and based largely on the pioneering work of economic strategist Harry S. Dent, Jr., this section focuses on the effects that demographic trends have on the broad economy. It is an essential read for anyone concerned about their financial future.

- Part II concerns the factors impacting state and local governments, specifically their employee and retiree healthcare funding liabilities. The funding requirements needed to finance promised healthcare benefits of the Baby Boomer generation will be the single biggest challenge for state and local governments for decades to come. Without an effective strategy to mitigate these liabilities, states, counties, and cities will find themselves under extreme financial duress…and with lots of attention from concerned taxpayers, employees, and retirees with which to contend. This section is highly recommended reading for state and local government officials and for anyone concerned with this impending crisis.

• Part III covers portfolio strategies for the years ahead. This section will advise on how to design appropriate portfolios and offers advice on which asset classes to favor in the next economic season. This will be valuable for anyone looking to protect and grow their wealth while minimizing risk.

• Finally, Part IV takes a look at the challenges and opportunities at the city, county, and state level due to changing demographic trends. In any economic season, there will be areas that prosper, at least relative to the national average, and other areas that lag behind. These chapters will be valuable to any current or aspiring homeowner, small business owner, or local public official. It should also prove valuable to young families planning their careers and to retirees considering a move. Special attention is given to California, the largest state in the union by population and economic clout.

Part I: It's All About *You*

Chapter 1: Demographics and the Economy

"All the world's a stage and all the men and women merely players."
—William Shakespeare's *As You Like It*

When Shakespeare penned the words above, the field of economics had not yet been invented. It would be nearly two more centuries until Adam Smith published *The Wealth of Nations*, but Shakespeare had already inadvertently grasped one of Smith's most important tenets: It is people that drive economies. In our careers, we each play our part by performing specialized tasks that are specific to our jobs; this is division of labor and specialization in "economist-speak", and it is what enables us to boost our productivity over time. We are not jacks of all trades, but instead masters of our own areas of expertise. This is progress.

This is not the only part we play in the economy, however. Not only are we producers; we are consumers. After all, there is not much point in going to work in the morning if not to support our lifestyles. We earn money to spend today, or we save it to spend later. But in any event, we earn it with a mind to eventually dispose of it.

We live in an economy dominated by consumer spending. In fact, it constitutes a full 70% of our annual GDP. This fact is a cause of concern for many economic commentators who associate consumption with waste. "Money should be saved and invested," the thinking goes, "as it is capital investment on the 'supply side' that drives economic growth."

It is the view of many today, as in Adam Smith's day, that savings and investment are virtues in of themselves. But, as Smith himself noted over 200 years ago, "*Consumption is the sole end and purpose of all*

3

production."[1] As individuals or as a country, we earn in order to spend. Our economic system is a means to this end.

Traditionally, there are two ways of explaining how an economy grows. A classical economist would insist that savings and investment in productive assets such as factories and equipment are what push the economy forward—"Supply creates its own demand," as Say's Law[2] says. "We have created something; therefore we can trade it to someone else."

"To the contrary," a Keynesian might retort. "What happens when there are no buyers for what you have to sell? Demand is the key. You can produce widgets all day long, but that doesn't mean that anyone will buy them. It is demand that spurs production."

In fact, both of these points of view are true to an extent. Production creates jobs, which provides income and gives the means for consumer spending, so classical economics is correct in this sense. Company profits are reinvested, allowing for the hiring of more workers, and the virtuous cycle continues. But the other side of the coin, Keynesian economics properly points out, is that consumers must make decisions on how that income is used. Will it be spent? Or will it be saved, stuffed under the mattress?

Both of these views attempt to explain the "how" of economic growth, but neither explains the "why." And both are focused disproportionately at the macro level. It is the micro level—the extreme micro level—where we find the answers.

Home Economics

The following section borrows heavily from the work of Harry S. Dent, Jr., who pioneered the use of demographics as an economic forecasting tool in his ground-breaking 1992 book *The Great Boom Ahead.* Dent is the first mainstream thinker to associate economic growth with the age structure of the population.

As stated previously, a full 70% of our economy is consumer spending, the daily shopping of the average American family[3]. The single

1 From *The Wealth of Nations*, Book IV

2 "Say's Law" is attributed to Jean-Baptiste Say (1767-1832), the noted French classical economist, and is a standard tenet of several schools of economic thought, including classical, neo-classical, supply-side, and Austrian.

3 See Bureau of Economic Analysis National Income and Product Tables (www.bea.gov)

biggest expense to this average family is, of course, children, and the older they get the more expensive they become. The U.S. Government estimates that the cost of raising a child born today from birth through high school to be $211,370[4]. Raising the standard two children would set an American family back nearly half a million dollars, and these figures do not take the cost of university education into account. It is this spending by families that drives our modern, mass-affluent economy. This spending continues even during very difficult times.

In the years between 2000 and 2008, Americans suffered through one of the worst bear markets in history in the wake of the dotcom bust, the worst terrorist attack in American history, two subsequent wars in Afghanistan and Iraq, and a hurricane that virtually destroyed a major American city. Yet despite the chaos, consumer spending actually rose every quarter before finally starting to plateau and fall slightly in 2008.

Are Americans blind to the world around them? Of course not. At worst, they can be accused of being stubbornly proud. Americans will do anything in their power to maintain their standards of living. Mom and Dad do not consider the trade deficit or the price/earnings ratio of the S&P 500 when Junior grows an inch and needs a new pair of jeans. As a general rule, people simply do not consider the macro economy when making household decisions. They may fret about the price of fuel around the water cooler at work, but when Junior needs a ride to soccer practice, Mom and Dad still buy that big SUV to get him there.

All the World's a Stage

People play very predictable roles in their lives. On average, people progress through a set of stages: marrying, having children, purchasing homes, and finally retiring in successive chapters of their lives. Understanding that this consumer life cycle exists, and then seeing how it can be forecast, is the key to understanding the economy, and even the stock market to a large extent.

By studying consumer purchasing data compiled by the U.S. Bureau of Labor Statistics Consumer Expenditure Survey we can forecast demand for hundreds of goods and services, including things as simple as potato chips. From this wealth of data, courtesy of the HS Dent Foundation,

---

4   Longman, Philip. *The Empty Cradle*

we know that the average American's spending on potato chips peaks at age 42 (see Figure 1.1). This can be expected, given that the average American married at about age 26, has a child at about age 28, and 14 years later that child is eating everything in sight.

Just as this type of forecasting can be done for individual products and services, it can also be done for aggregate household spending. Total household consumer spending tops out when the breadwinner hits his or her late 40s or early 50s, just as the average child is leaving home.

Potato Chip Purchases By Age

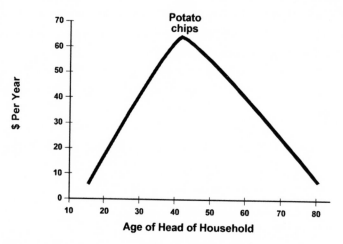

Source: HS Dent Foundation, from data provided by the Consumer Expenditure Survey

Figure 1.1 – Spending on Potato Chips by Age

"Demogranomics"

Every year since the early 1980s the U.S. Bureau of Labor Statistics has conducted the Consumer Expenditure Survey, asking thousands of respondents to keep a record of all their purchases. Along with their purchases, we also know something about the respondents themselves, such as age, income, marital status, education, etc. So, as in the example above, we know how much money, on average, an American of each age spends on potato chips. We know that this spending peaks, on average, at age 42.

All that is lacking to build an accurate forecasting model of potato chip demand is the age distribution of our population. By knowing whether the number of 42 year olds is growing or contracting, we can forecast rising or falling demand for potato chips. The same is true for the other products and services that have predictable demand patterns by age and for aggregate consumer spending as a whole. To determine how many people are at each age, we turn again to the U.S. Government for figures.

The National Center for Health Statistics reports how many babies are born in each year. Adding immigrants by their birth year to these statistics give us the Immigration-Adjusted Birth Index (Figure 1.2), courtesy of the HS Dent Foundation. The large bulge in the chart starting around 1938 and peaking in 1961 is, of course, the Baby Boomer generation.

Immigration Adjusted Birth Index

Source: HS Dent Foundation, from data provided by the National Center for Health Statistics and the INS

Figure 1.2: Immigration-Adjusted Birth Index

Knowing, as we now do, the average age of the buyer for hundreds of products and services, we can project the demand for any of those products by lagging the Immigration Adjusted Birth Index by the appropriate number of years. Take college education, for example.

Why is it so difficult to get into many colleges today? Look at Figure 1.2 for the number of people born 18 years ago—1990—and the growth of the curve leading up to that birth year. It is no coincidence that college tuition has skyrocketed in recent years; the shear number of 18-22 year-olds has overwhelmed the system as those children born from 1976 through 1990 keep pouring in. Forecasting the demand for college entry would simply mean moving forward Figure 1.2 by 18 years (adding 18 to the numbers across the x-axis), as depicted in Figure 1.3. Simple, and yet very powerful.

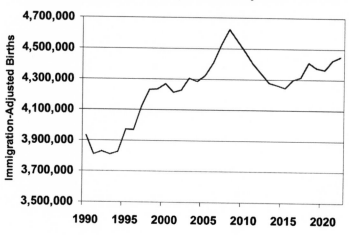

Source: HS Dent Foundation

Figure 1.3: College Entry Demand

We can also use this same methodology to forecast aggregate demand across the economy. As mentioned above, a person's consumer spending tends to level off around age 46 and then actually decline after age 50. So, pushing the Birth Index forward by 48 years, in the middle of the range, gives us a good, long-term forecasting model of consumer demand. This model, dubbed the Spending Wave, was created by Harry Dent in the early 1990s and has been refined over the years. It is not designed to predict every twist and turn in the economy or every miniscule revision to quarterly GDP; it is not going to tell you every time Wal-Mart or Home Depot will have a bad quarter or every time Congress will allocate funds for a major new initiative. But it *is* an excellent model for forecasting the "big picture." It *will* tell you the general direction of consumer spending growth and, ultimately, the economy. This is, quite possibly, the most powerful long-term forecasting model constructed to date, and unlike the noise that bombards us every day in the newspapers and on TV, this is practical information that can be used in real personal and business planning.

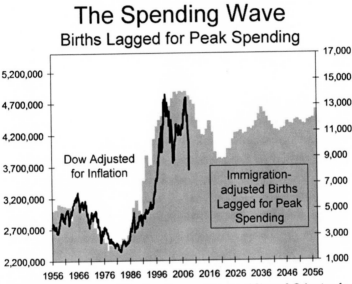

The Spending Wave
Births Lagged for Peak Spending

Figure 1.4: Spending Wave

The "Me" Generation

Though ridiculed by social commentators as the "Me" Generation, the Baby Boomers might be forgiven for believing the world revolves around them because for much of the past 50 years, the economic world really *has* revolved around them.

The Boomers have been a proverbial "bull in a china shop" over the course of their lives, radically disrupting the world economy with their shear size. This generation—perhaps more than any other in history—has truly defined our age. Their births in the years following

9

World War II heralded the massive expansion of the American suburbs, as their parents needed bigger homes in which to raise them. The surge in the number of school-aged children necessitated school construction on a massive, unprecedented scale. As they become teenagers and young adults, the rock & roll culture they created led to cultural and social revolution. (Ironically, as parents today many of aging Boomers would love to curtail the libertine youth culture that they themselves created in their formative years.)

In the 1970s, the largest generation in history began to enter the workforce en masse. Not shockingly, the entry of millions of young, untrained workers led to the biggest eruption of peacetime inflation in American history (more on this in Chapter 3). As Boomer workers gained experience in the 1980s, productivity surged, inflation fell, and the economy reached new highs. The 1980s "Decade of Greed" was largely a result of the Boomers "getting haircuts and real jobs," rolling up their sleeves, and getting to work. Similarly, the technology revolution of the 1990s was largely the result of the innovations of Boomers like Apple Computer founder Steve Jobs and Microsoft founder Bill Gates that went mainstream.

The Baby Boomers' effect on our economy and society has been compared to "a pig passing though a python" and for good reason. So, what does this generation have in store for us now?

As we see in Figure 1.4, the prosperity that started with the Reagan Revolution in the early 1980s corresponded to a change in direction of the Spending Wave. This is not a coincidence. President Ronald Reagan's reforms might have unleashed the productive capacity of the country, but someone had to actually buy that production. Reagan unleashed the country's supply side, but it was the Spending Wave that functioned as the demand side. (Reagan also had to get *elected* in the first place. As the Boomers reached early middle age, they also became more conservative and economically libertarian in their politics, eschewing the radical views of their youth. But as these same Boomers mature into late middle age and into their golden years, they are likely to become even more culturally conservative in their politics but also far more in favor of government safety nets when it comes to social programs like Social Security and Medicare, thus changing the direction of American politics yet again.)

Figure 1.4 shows that the Spending Wave levels off at around 2009. Of course, we have already technically been in recession since late 2007. The collapse of the housing market and ensuing credit crisis appear to have pulled the tipping point forward by a little over a year. Economic winter came a little early this season.

But what does this actually mean? What exactly does the downward slope of the Spending Wave look like? For our best estimate, we look east.

The Land of the Setting Sun

Japan was truly the first modern "miracle" economy in the years following World War II. No country in history could match Japan's growth rates from the 1950s through the 1970s. In just two decades, Japan evolved from a largely agrarian country to an industrial powerhouse that rivaled the United States. By the 1980s, Americans suddenly found themselves struggling to compete with Japanese manufactures in steel, autos, and consumer electronics. The Japanese stock market played its part in the affair. Share prices shot through the roof in the 1980s, and by the middle of the decade were in a speculative bubble. Between 1985 and 1990 the Nikkei tripled, hitting a high just shy of 40,000 in December of 1989.

Not to be outdone, the Japanese real estate bubble dwarfed that of the stock market. Home prices in Tokyo far outpaced incomes, making 100-year multigenerational mortgages a necessity. At its peak, Japanese property was worth four times that of the entire United States. The area around the Imperial Palace alone was gauged to be more valuable than the state of California, Silicon Valley and all.

Today, we see a very different Japan. The Nikkei is still down over 70% from the top, nearly two decades later! Japan has spent the last two decades in and out of recession, unable to gain any real momentum. So what caused Japan to fall into this long, dark economic hibernation? As you might guess, it was largely the falling desire of Japanese consumers. Low consumer demand due to the aging of the population meant low profits for Japanese companies, which in turn led to decreased hiring and even lower demand. A vicious cycle developed with no way out. In the wake of the 2008 credit crisis, this cycle—lower demand, lower profits, lower production, lower demand, etc.—may already be underway in the United States as well.

But surely nothing like that could happen in the United States. Fed Chairman Ben Bernanke has effectively lowered the Federal Funds target rate to zero. The Bush Administration has launched the biggest fiscal stimulus drive in history, and the incoming Obama Administration has promised to do much the same. Would this not save us from falling into a deflationary trap like Japan? Unfortunately, the historical precedent suggests that it will not.

As the Japanese crisis wore on, the Bank of Japan cut interest rates from 6% to zero, essentially giving money away in the hopes that someone would spend it. In the standard monetarist formula, lowering interest rates spurs both consumption and investment. As the reward for saving money gets smaller, the incentive to spend it or invest it gets bigger. But an odd thing happened in Japan; interest rates dropped, but savings remained high. Consumer spending stayed flat and then fell. New investment in productive assets stalled; Japanese businesses already had more than enough capacity. In the 1930s, John Maynard Keynes likened this kind of situation to "pushing on a string." It could also be compared to herding cats. Injecting liquidity into the system and making money available to lend is useless if no one is interested in borrowing.

Japan did not stop with central bank monetary policy, of course. The government launched countless fiscal stimulus programs, most of which barely made a blip on the radar screen. Much like the Roosevelt Administration during the Depression, the Japanese used massive government deficit spending to spur demand, but the Japanese did this on an even bigger scale. The once fiscally conservative Japanese government went on the largest public works spending spree in history, boosting its budget deficits and government debts to levels rarely seen in developed countries. Today, Japan has 30 times the amount of land covered in concrete as the United States, adjusting for the size difference in the two countries, and over 2,800 river dams, but the Japanese version of the Tennessee Valley Authority could not possibly hope to spend enough money to compensate for a lack of private consumer spending.

We see the United States going though a similar process. The next decade should be one of slow or even mildly negative economic growth. U.S. policymakers have thus far succeeded in not making the mistakes made by their predecessors during the Great Depression, when Andrew Mellon, Secretary of the Treasury, recommended to "liquidate labor, liquidate stocks, liquidate the farmers, liquidate real estate…purge the rottenness out of the system."

No Republican or Democrat would echo Secretary Mellon's advice today, as they now know where that road leads. Both political parties have agreed to do whatever is necessary to keep the financial system afloat. A slow-motion depression like that of 1990s Japan is the more likely scenario. So what does that scenario look like?

From 1990s until the present, Japan's population continued to age, with the bulk of the Japanese Baby Boomers advancing past their peak spending years. The result was a stretch of nearly two decades in which consumer spending failed to materially rise. Japanese companies found their home markets saturated and thus had to rely ever more heavily on exports. Meanwhile, Japanese stock and home prices continued to drift inexorably lower.

History never repeats itself exactly, but, to paraphrase Mark Twain, it does tend to rhyme. Demographic trends point to a continued erosion of home values in most U.S. cities. As for stocks, the picture is more complex. American stocks fell so far and so fast in 2008, further downside may be somewhat limited. Popular valuation metrics, such as the price/earnings ratio, are at levels not seen in decades.

But while stocks may be cheap by modern standards, this is no guarantee that they represent a good long-term value at these levels. The Spending Wave tells us that consumer spending growth will be slow at best for roughly the next decade. Housing prices are likely to continue falling as well, meaning that the crisis currently facing U.S. banks is not likely to improve. At current prices, there is clearly less risk in the market than there was a year ago, and returns over the next decade could prove to be positive. "Positive" does not necessarily mean "big," however, and we believe that stock price returns will be modest at best. We would recommend concentrating investor portfolios in solid, income-producing assets and in basic infrastructure industries that are likely to benefit from government spending in the developed world and from growth in emerging markets.

Chapter 2: Demographics and the Economy, Part II[5]

The late Milton Friedman may be the most accomplished economist of his generation. Just as his predecessor John Maynard Keynes influenced every aspect of economic thinking and policy in the 1930s, 40s, and 50s, virtually every significant development in recent decades towards free and open markets bears Friedman's mark. Friedman's Chicago School provided much of the intellectual fuel for the Reagan and Thatcher Revolutions in America and Britain. General Augusto Pinochet staffed his government with "Chicago Boys," as Friedman's students were called, who eventually gave Chile one of the most competitive economies in the developing world. Milton Friedman was a revolutionary who changed the world, though this chapter is not about his intellectual exploits. Rather, it explains the economist's theories on consumer behavior and relates them to our own research and to the demographic insights of Harry S. Dent, Jr. We will attempt here to use the work of Friedman and others to discuss the implications for the years ahead.

But First, a Word on Keynes...

Any discussion of consumption must first start with a review of John Maynard Keynes and his work. Pre-Keynes, most economic theory was focused on production, or the supply side of the equation. Consumption, driven by end-user demand, was merely an afterthought, something that just "happened" and didn't need to be explained. This was best summarized by Say's Law, which we briefly mentioned in the last chapter. Say's Law is a maxim memorized by every freshman economics student: "Supply creates its own demand." By virtue of manufacturing something, you have created a demand for that something, since it can

---

5   This chapter appeared in the August 2007 issue of the *HS Dent Forecast* under the title "Milton Friedman and HS Dent" and has been modified and expanded for this book.

15

be traded for other goods. This could be called a "build it and they will come" strategy, to borrow a line from the movie *Field of Dreams*.

But what happens when supply *doesn't* create its own demand? What happens—as in the Great Depression and in 1990s Japan—there is not sufficient demand to absorb a plentiful supply?

During the Great Depression in the United States and United Kingdom, consumers stopped consuming, virtually snapping their wallets shut for more than a decade. This lead Keynes to his study of consumer behavior, which is best summarized by his Consumption Function (also required memorization by freshmen econ students), seen below in Figure 2.1.

The Consumption Function

$$C = c_0 + c_1 Y^d$$

c_0 = baseline consumption on necessities

Y^d = income

c_1 = "marginal propensity to consume," or the percentage of your income that you spend.

Figure 2.1: Consumption Function

Keynes's formula says that people spend a constant percentage of their current incomes, once basic necessities are provided. So, the average American cashes his paycheck every two weeks and spends, say, 75% of that paycheck each and every pay period of his life. When he gets a raise and his check rises, he spends 75% of the now higher amount. When times are hard and he takes a pay cut, he instantly cuts his spending down to 75% of the new, smaller, amount. The average American's spending is completely flexible and based solely on his current income.

Of course, this is obviously false, both for individuals and for entire economies. To start, most consumption in the modern economy is not really "discretionary." Most significant expenditures—everything from the home mortgage to piano lessons for your son or daughter—are paid on some kind of monthly payment plan. Even though piano lessons can be stopped at any time, they generally aren't. Likewise, your cable TV plan does not get upgraded to the deluxe, high-definition package one month and then get cut to basic cable or—gasp!—rabbit ears the next. Your cable bill is stable and changes only slightly over time.

Most expenses are very slow to change when income changes. One of the major benefits of the modern credit-driven economy is that it can provide for *lifestyle stability*. If money is a little tight this month, your family's lifestyle does not have to radically change, at least not immediately. This is the primary reason that consumer spending is so resilient despite economic calamity and why economists have been consistently wrong in their forecasting of recessions.

Keynes also fails to note that spending and saving habits are affected by level of wealth and—most importantly to our research—age and stage of life (see Figure 2.2, courtesy of the HS Dent Foundation). We'll give credit to Keynes for being the first person to approach consumption scientifically, but it is obvious that his model was incomplete and not reflective of the real world.

Change in Spending at each Age & Stage of Life

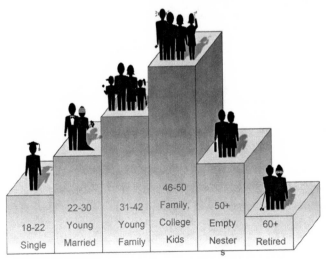

Source: HS Dent Foundation

Figure 2.2: Ages and Stages of Life

Many of these deficiencies were addressed by the economists Modigliani, Brumberg, and Ando in the 1950s and 60s in what became known as the Life Cycle Hypothesis (Figure 2.3). These economists graphically displayed what every household intuitively knows. People follow a life cycle of earning and spending. In early career, our incomes are low relative to our expenses, often forcing us to take out large debts for homes, cars, appliances, etc. In middle age, we earn enough money to meet all of our current expenses, plus save for retirement. In retirement our income falls and we slowly spend down our savings.

Life Cycle Hypothesis

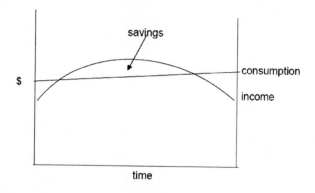

Source: Stevens, 2004

Figure 2.3: Life Cycle

This model, though more advanced than Keynes's, is still problematic. Notice in Figure 2.3 that income makes a curve while consumption makes a straight line. This chart is suggesting that our consumer spending increases in a mild, linear fashion from birth until death. Again, we know from Harry Dent's insights that this is also false. Spending follows a curve much like that of income, though on a different timeline. Consider Figure 2.4, what we will call the "HS Dent Modified Life Cycle."

In this case, the income line has the same basic shape as in Figure 2.3, though the consumption line has been transformed into a curve. This should look familiar, as it is a replication of Figure 2.5.

HS Dent Modified Life Cycle Hypothesis

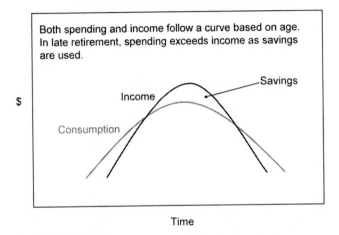

Source: HS Dent Foundation

Figure 2.4: HS Dent Modified Life Cycle Hypothesis

Household Spending By Age

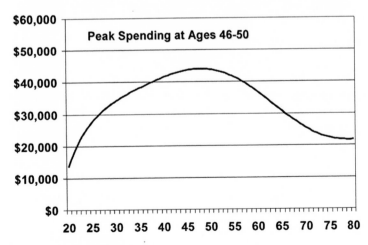

Source: Bureau of Labor Statistics

Figure 2.5: Household Spending By Age

This chart is the basis for the Spending Wave, discussed in Chapter 1. We know, based on data from the U.S. Bureau of Labor Statistics, that consumer spending is a function of age. We spend increasingly more raising our families until our late 40s or early 50s, after which time we pare down our spending and save for retirement. We'll return to this theme shortly.

The Permanent Income Hypothesis

In 1957, Milton Friedman made his own modifications to the Consumption Function and to the Life Cycle Hypothesis, dubbed the Permanent Income Hypothesis. Friedman's idea was that people base their consumer spending on what they consider their "permanent" income, or their average income over time. They do this in an attempt to maintain a relatively constant standard of living, even though their incomes may vary wildly over time. This goes a long way to explaining why Americans love consumer debt as much as they do. It's ok to spend more that you make today, because your salary will be high enough after that next promotion to pay it all back.

Keynes's model assumed that people spent a constant proportion of their *current* incomes, i.e. each paycheck. Friedman assumes that people are forward-looking and base consumption decisions today on income expectations for tomorrow. Changes in current income, if perceived to be temporary, have little effect on spending. Friedman correctly realized that a family's standard of living is "sticky." When dad's bonus check is a little disappointing one year, the family does not instantly eschew Neiman Marcus in favor of Wal-Mart (the 2008 holiday shopping season notwithstanding). Whether for pride, concern for their children, or simple inertia, Americans are slow to ratchet down their lifestyles.

Figure 2.6 shows how resilient American consumers have been. There was an occasional down month in consumer spending, but the uptrend was never broken. Keynes might have despaired that this behavior was irrational, but under Friedman's model there is nothing irrational about it at all. American consumers are simply optimists who, seeing better times in the future, decide to enjoy the benefits of consumption today.

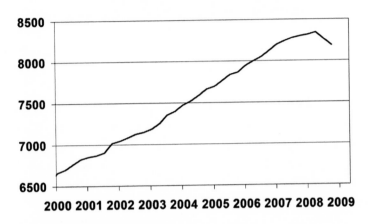

Real Personal Consumption Expenditures Jan 2000 – Dec 2008

Source: Bureau of Economic Analysis

Figure 2.6: Personal Consumption Expenditures

The Other Side of the Coin

Interestingly, none of these theories go into much detail on consumption as a function of age and what this implies in an aging society. Keynes's model does not incorporate time at all, and the Life Cycle theorists and Milton Friedman both assume that consumption rises in a linear fashion from birth to death. Keynes's model may be the least problematic in this sense, as nothing is as destructive to a forecasting model as this kind of linear thinking. The tendency to project current conditions into infinity leads to booms and busts. Remember the dotcom boom? It seems ridiculous now, but professional investors implicitly assumed that growth rates that were *far* in excess of historical norms would continue indefinitely into the future: "Our website is attracting 100,000 new eyeballs per day...." The housing bubble and subsequent collapse in California, Florida, and parts of Nevada and Arizona is another painful reminder of the dangers of linear thinking.

Milton Friedman was an optimist and a true believer in the market system, and these are some of his most memorable and endearing qualities. They are what allowed him to spread his views so effectively and radically change the world for the better. It is only natural, in Friedman's optimistic opinion, for consumer spending to march upward more or less continuously with only mild setbacks here and there. But we know that this is not true. People do indeed increase their spending for most of their lives, but once they hit their 50s (or their children leave the nest) they spend less on virtually everything but healthcare.

Friedman is partially right, of course. A person's income and expectation of future income clearly affects the level of consumption today. A janitor is not likely to buy a Porsche, because at no time in his life will his income justify such a purchase. But how many Porsches (or boats, or expensive clothes, or Rolex watches) do you see 70-year-old retirees buying?

These are luxury goods, of course. But what about more mundane items? How many washing machines, sofas, or coffee machines does a 70-year-old retiree buy? Common sense would tell you that the answer is "not very many." Is the reason, as Friedman's hypothesis would suggest, because the retiree realizes that his or her future income with which to pay for these items is modest? Or might it be for the more obvious reason that the retiree has already accumulated more than enough of these things in his or her 70 years of life?

Demographic trends suggest a decade-long lull in consumer spending starting around 2008 to 2010 as the Baby Boomers begin to spend less and save more for retirement. The housing and credit crisis of 2007-2008 appears to have sped this process up and may in retrospect be the "high-water mark" for the U.S. economy and markets for years, if not decades, to come. Again, it is too early to say conclusively, but we may already be entering a long-term, deflationary cooling period that could see economic growth and corporate profits stagnate and stock P/E ratios further compress.

If so, this will be a repeat, almost twenty years later, of the same scenario that Japan faced during the 1990s. When U.S. consumer spending begins to falter, there will no doubt be plenty of economists attempting to explain the phenomenon by using some variation of Friedman's permanent income hypothesis: "Americans are spending less money today because they see dark economic times ahead with declining incomes and standards of living...." Then, any and every policy under the sun will be recommended on how to "fix" the problem. No doubt, Keynes's Depression-era work will also be resurrected, and phrases like "liquidity trap" will become popular again in economic circles.

None of these ideas are likely to make much difference in spurring demand. They certainly did not in Japan, and there was no lack of trying. Japan eventually recovered, as the United States will too. But the recovery in demand was a result of changes in demographic trends, not a public policy decision.

Chapter 3: Inflation or Deflation Ahead?[6]

Inflation was a popular word in the mid-2000s, seeming to pop up everywhere. "Googling" the word will result in over 50 *million* hits. A cursory reading of the *Wall Street Journal* or the minutes from the Federal Reserve governors' meetings of the past year will also show the popularity of the word. The massive amount of fiscal and monetary stimulus coming out of Congress and the Federal Reserve in the assorted "bailouts" have also generated fears of "Weimar-style" hyperinflation. After more than two decades in the shadows, it appears that inflation has finally become newsworthy again. It's been blamed for the rising price of oil, gold, and real estate. It's been blamed for the falling dollar and a hyper-aggressive Federal Reserve. After enjoying 25 years of moderating inflation, has the trend finally reversed? Do we face a future of rising prices and falling living standards?

Some of the most respected minds in finance would say exactly that—and they would use demographics to make their cases. Both Ben Bernanke, Chairman of the Federal Reserve, and Jeremy Siegel, the respected Wharton professor and best-selling financial author, have written extensively on the economic effects of the retirement of the Baby Boomers, the largest generation in history. Both discuss inflation and describe a scenario much like the 1970s. No, Messrs. Bernanke and Siegel are not predicting a comeback for handlebar mustaches, earth tones, and shag carpet. But they do see a return of that *other* scourge of the disco decade: stagflation.

While we agree with the "stag" part of the forecast (economic stagnation), we would have to differ on the "flation" outlook. Sure, there will be a "flation" coming. But we believe that *de*flation—not *in*flation—will be the primary threat in the next decade.

This debate is not academic. It is very real, and there are serious

---

6   This article originally in the January 2007 issue of the HS Dent Forecast. It has been updated and substantially expanded for this book.

financial consequences for those that are unprepared. A financial plan designed to survive and profit during inflationary times is fundamentally different from one designed for deflationary times. Ask anyone who lived through the inflationary 1970s or the ultra-deflationary Great Depression of the 1930s. Having a mortgage in the 1970s was great; every year the debt you owed became less valuable and your home more valuable, as inflation eroded the value of the dollar and thus your mortgage debt. The 1970s were the ultimate bailout for debtors. If you had lived during the 1930s, however, your situation would have been exactly the opposite. Your debt would have remained large in current dollars while the value of your property plummeted. It would have been a quick path to bankruptcy, and in fact it was for many home and business owners. So knowing what type of environment to expect—inflationary or deflationary—is critical when planning your financial future.

A Little Background

Most people are familiar with inflation and how it impacts their lives. The Big Mac that costs a dollar today might cost $1.10 next year. Customers will be paying a higher price for the exact same product; this is inflation. McDonalds has not necessarily made more profit, however, because their labor and supply prices have also risen. Prices have risen across the board, including—hopefully—your own income.

But what if the Big Mac actually falls next year to $0.90? We then have deflation, which is great if you're the one buying the hamburger (as long as your income has not fallen as well). It's not so great if you're the one selling the hamburger. Suddenly, your revenue just fell. This puts pressure on McDonalds to keep its wages low and squeeze lower prices out of its suppliers. Those suppliers in turn have to cut their own costs, including wages to workers. The end result is lower prices, stagnant or falling wages, and higher unemployment spreading throughout the economy, and that is just the beginning. When business owners see falling prices, they refrain from expanding their businesses. Why would they invest their money today in building a new factory or office building if the price of the good or service they intend to sell is actually falling?

Once deflation sets in, it becomes a vicious cycle that can prove almost impossible to break. As a consumer, why would you buy a new car today if you knew you could buy that same car next year for 10% less? And why would you risk spending any money at all if you feared your own paycheck might shrink? The *fear* of deflation becomes a self-fulfilling prophecy, and economic activity grinds to a halt. As unpleasant as inflation is, it is the fear of deflation that keeps Fed Chairmen awake at night. Before taking the job, Ben Bernanke was known infamously as "Helicopter Ben" for comments made about deflation. To paraphrase, Mr. Bernanke said, only half joking, that the Federal Reserve would do *anything* in its power to avoid deflation, even if it meant literally dumping dollars out of helicopters in the hopes that someone would spend them. It is also worth mentioning that Franklin Delano Roosevelt's most famous speech was in reference to the sentiment that falling prices caused. The "fear" most eloquently described in "*The only thing we have to fear is fear itself*" was not of the Nazi regime gaining power in Germany. No, Roosevelt was referring instead to the vicious cycle of pessimism brought on by deflation, going on to call it a *"nameless, unreasoning, unjustified terror which paralyzes needed efforts to convert retreat into advance."*[7]

So what causes inflation and deflation? There are two basic mainstream views, Keynesian and monetarist, pioneered by John Maynard Keynes and Milton Friedman, respectively. Other, more unorthodox views have used demographics to explain inflation and deflation. Thus far, the best demographic arguments have been made by David Hackett Fischer and Gregory Clark for pre-industrial economies and by Harry S. Dent, Jr. for post-industrial, mass-affluent societies. As noted, Fed Chairman Ben Bernanke and Jeremy Siegel also offered some insights on the matter. We'll examine each of these views in the pages that follow.

Econ 101

John Maynard Keynes was the first real "celebrity" economist, and regrettably not the last (Lord Keynes would have been a frequent guest on CNBC, had it existed in his day, and perhaps even Oprah).

---

7   Franklin D. Roosevelt, Inaugural Address, March 4, 1933

Adam Smith made the social rounds in Enlightenment-era Scotland, of course, but the discipline of economics itself had yet to rise to the near mystical status it achieved during Lord Keynes's lifetime.

Keynes rose to prominence in the difficult economic times of the 1920s and 1930s and was the first economist to focus on the demand side of the equation. Prior to Keynes, supply was the only real consideration among economists, with demand as nothing more than an afterthought. In fact, as mentioned in previous chapters, one of the foundations of pre-Keynes classical economics was Say's Law: "supply creates its own demand." In other words, by supplying hamburgers, McDonalds has created demand for cars from General Motors. After all, the McDonalds workers and managers need to get to work, and with regular paychecks they have the means. GM auto production in turn leads to demand for McDonalds burgers. Auto workers have to eat. Production leads to consumption.

Lord Keynes turned Say's Law upside down. What is the benefit of production if there is no demand for the finished product due to lack of money or lack or interest? What if there is too much supply for a given level of demand? What if you simply choose to save your money rather than spend it?

In the Keynesian view, inflation happens when aggregate demand outstrips aggregate supply. In other words, when we want to consume more than we are capable of producing, the prices rise in the marketplace. On the flip side, when we produce more than we want or need prices fall, leading to deflation. Likewise, when we indulge in speculative bubbles and build far more railroad track, office towers, or fiber optic cable than would be economically justified (as happened in the 1870s, 1980s and 1990s, respectively), prices plummet and the boom turns to bust. No new investment is needed until demand catches up to supply.

Keynes believed that an economy could remain in a state of overcapacity and deflation for a very long time. His solution was to create artificial demand via government spending to "mop up" the excess production and labor during the periods when production outstrips demand. While we agree with Keynes that an economy can stay underutilized for extended periods of time, we would argue that government spending is not a viable solution, at least not for long-term, secular declines. We'll return to this point later.

The Chicago Boys

The other mainstream view of inflation and deflation is that of the monetarist school, led by the late Milton Freedman, patriarch of the Chicago School of economic thought. Friedman proposed that changes in the price level (aka inflation and deflation) are almost purely effects of monetary policy by the Federal Reserve. One of Friedman's most quoted statements was: *"Inflation is always and everywhere a monetary phenomenon."* In this line of thinking, if the Fed "prints" more money than is needed to make the economy function, the value of that money decreases and the price of everything rises. Hence, we have inflation. On the flip side, if the Fed fails to print enough money, we have a "shortage" of cash, and prices fall: deflation. This is loosely the view of Fed Chairman Ben Bernanke, and there is certainly a lot of truth to it. Central banks are certainly capable of creating artificial inflation or deflation. It wasn't that long ago that Brazil had an inflation rate of over 1,000% per year, and when referring to U.S. economic history both Friedman and Bernanke have mentioned that unnecessarily high interest rates by the Fed were a major contributing factor to the deflation of the Great Depression. It appears that central banks can get monetary policy wrong in either direction, causing inflation or deflation as the case might be.

Friedman is correct; a central bank *can* affect the money supply. A central bank *cannot*, however, increase the *velocity* of money, or the frequency with which a dollar changes hands in the economy. As Keynes correctly pointed out, in the absence of underlying demand, stimulative monetary policy (aka printing more money) is akin to "pushing on a string." Simply having more money around does not guarantee that it will be spent.

Demographics: The Inflation of People

In his 1996 book *The Great Wave*, David Hackett Fischer describes the last 1,000 years of human history as a series of price revolutions caused by demographic shifts. The basic pattern is like so: increases in productivity lead to stability and higher real incomes, which encourages population growth. Population growth means more mouths to feed, which means the farming of marginal land to produce more food. Farming on marginal, lower-quality land reduces productivity, which leads to rising prices for food (inflation). Rising food prices leads to chaos and instability as rival factions vie for control over limited resources.

A large labor force and small returns on labor lead to falling real wages, lower standards of living, unrest, substance abuse, illegitimate births, and a general breakdown of society. In this environment, medieval landlords were the only people to do well, as they benefited from rising rents on their land. This leads to greater inequality and social unrest, which usually results in political instability and a reduction in the birthrate. As population falls and marginal land is no longer used, productivity goes up, real incomes go up, and returns to capital go down. This increases the wealth of the labor force but causes financial strain for landlords, resulting in greater equality between social classes.

So, in the pre-industrial world, life got much worse for the common man during inflationary times and actually quite a bit better during deflationary times. Meanwhile, the exact opposite was true for the landlords, or the rich. The propertied class did well during inflationary times and fell under severe financial distress during deflationary times. So, by this logic, we should welcome deflation, right? After all, if only a small minority of the ultra-affluent suffer, what's the big deal?

The problem with this argument is that the modern middle-class American has a lot more in common with the medieval landlord than with the medieval common man. In the modern, mass-affluent economy, we all have the trappings of the rich. We have mortgages to pay and assets to protect. We no longer live in the Malthusian world described above in which the ability to afford food is the most pressing concern for the mass of humanity.

This brings us to the work of another economic historian, Gregory Clark, author of *A Farewell to Alms*. Clark explains at length the dynamics of the "Malthusian" economy, named after Thomas Malthus, the English demographer and thinker who predicted that mankind would face mass starvation by the middle of the 19ᵗʰ century. (These views were resurrected about a century later by the neo-Malthusian Paul Ehrlich in his book *The Population Bomb*. Both proved to be wrong for reasons to be discussed.)

In the Malthusian world of scarcity, mankind survived at just above the subsistence level. Any increase in productivity would result in higher incomes, which would result in higher birthrates. The increased number of people would push income back to the subsistence level. If, due to a famine, war, crop failure, etc., income fell below the subsistence level, people would have fewer children and would suffer higher mortality rates. The weakest among us would be the first to die until our populations were thinned out enough to make subsistence living possible again. In this Darwinian world of "survival of the fittest," disease, pestilence, death, and destruction were perversely the best friends of the healthy among us. If a bout of plague hit a given region and wiped out 30% of the population, all of the survivors saw their respective pieces of the income pie get 30% larger. Fewer mouths to feed meant more food for the rest of us!

Luckily, the Industrial Revolution pulled us out of this cycle. For the first time in human history, ordinary people had the ability to generate real wealth and live in a society of abundance, not scarcity. Rising populations meant more production, better division of labor, more specialization, and higher standards of living. In the mass-affluent society that emerged, larger populations meant more consumers, more people to buy what you have to sell. "More" finally meant "better," unless you were a parent. A large family suddenly became a very expensive luxury rather than a survival need.

Both Fischer and Clark implicitly take a view of inflation that is consistent with Keynes's work and with the work of the classical economists. Prices rise and fall as supply and demand shift. Like Keynes, these men focus mostly on the "demand side" of the equation, supply being limited to the arable land available to grow food. "Supply side" economics is meaningless in a pre-industrial, agrarian world of low productivity growth.

Inflation in the Era of Mass Affluence

Let us return for a moment to Milton Friedman and the monetarist school. In light of the analysis above, we view Friedman's work as incomplete. While Fed monetary policy can and does have an impact on the economy and on the level of prices, other factors, such as demographics, clearly play significant roles as well, particularly in the velocity of money. Lowering the Fed Funds rate when there is no underlying source of demand is "pushing on a string." It can *release* pent-up demand, but it can't *create* it.

We would have to agree with Lord Keynes and respectfully disagree with Mr. Friedman on this issue. We do, however, want to add an important caveat here: John Maynard Keynes's work has become associated with socialism and state control of the economy, not to mention rampant government spending and debt. Milton Friedman, in contrast, is associated with libertarian, free-market economics with minimum state intervention. Philosophically, we favor the Friedman view of free-market capitalism, not only because it creates the best broad incentives for innovation, but because it is counterproductive to try to "eliminate" economic cycles. Booms and bust allow for "creative destruction," in Joseph Schumpeter's words. Booms allow for new ideas to be tested; busts cause weaker ideas to fail. The result is that our economy evolves in a Darwinian survival of the fittest. However, it just so happens that on the particular issues of inflation and deflation, the Keynesian view is closer to reality. In short, we agree with Keynes's analysis of the issues even if we do not agree with his solutions.

That said, we also believe that Keynes's view is incomplete because he fails to explain the root *causes* of the changes in aggregate supply and demand that lead to inflation and deflation. Luckily, more recent research has filled in some of these gaps. In the early 1990s, Harry S. Dent, Jr. took the inflation/deflation debate in an entirely new direction. We will summarize his views below.

In a developed, service-based economy such as that of the United States, labor is by far the biggest and most significant expense on the supply side of the equation. In order for an employee to be viable, they must produce more in output than they cost in wages. Unfortunately, new workers produce very little in their first few months or years, yet they still have to be paid. They also need a desk and a computer or machine tools and a hard hat, not to mention office or factory space and possibly even a company car or mobile phone. And we haven't even mentioned fringe benefits such as health insurance and continuing education classes that add to the cost of each employee. Suffice it to say, new employees are expensive and initially produce very little relative to their costs.

This means that when a new employee is hired, the company's expenses instantly rise but with little or no change in production. When this happens on a large scale, we have inflation. And of course, inflation doesn't start at employment. Young people require a massive investment to raise and educate, from both their parents and the government, for their entire pre-working lives. Hence, young people are inflationary from birth (or even sooner, given the rising cost of pre-natal care) until they enter the workforce and start to produce more than they cost (typically two to three years after entry). We can even take this one step further: when a career woman becomes a mother and takes maternity leave, she is temporarily removed from her normal productive capacities at work. This means that the company continues to have expenses while getting no production. This also says nothing of the lost productivity of mothers and fathers alike from the sleepless nights of attending to a crying baby or a sick toddler. We could continue this train of thought almost indefinitely to make our point: children are inflationary from birth until early career.

Of course, this is not a bad thing. Children are a necessary investment in the future. New workers eventually become highly productive, and their human capital becomes an asset to the company that hires them. Perhaps more importantly, fresh talent brings new ideas and innovations. Often times, the full benefits of these innovations are not realized for decades. Consider personal computers. The key innovations in this product were made by Steve Jobs and Bill Gates in their respective companies in the early 1980s, but the resulting revolution in productivity did not happen until the mid-1990s. Companies and individuals invested millions (if not billions) of dollars before they began to truly realize a payoff.

In this context, inflation can be thought of as a means of financing new generations and the new technologies that they bring. Innovation and inflation go hand in hand.

In 1989, Harry Dent found a strong correlation between inflation and workforce growth rates on a three-year lag. Figure 3.1 shows that correlation, courtesy of the HS Dent Foundation. There is obviously a fair amount of "noise" in the graph, but the trend is clear. In the 1960s and 1970s, rising workforce entry by the Baby Boomers caused rising inflation rates. Since the 1980s, we have seen disinflation (which is falling inflation rates as opposed to deflation, which is negative inflation rates), as the Boomers and their new technologies have matured and become highly productive.

HS Dent Inflation Indicator

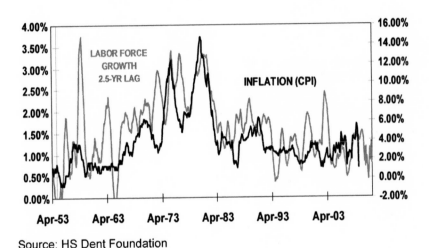

Source: HS Dent Foundation

Figure 3.1: Dent Inflation Indicator

A slightly different methodology would be to simply to lag the Birth Index (described in Chapter 1) by 20-24 years, creating the Inflation/Innovation Wave. We will explore that method in a later chapter when we compare inflation forecasts for various countries around the world.

Using the methodology of Figure 3.1, we can make long-term inflation projections. Dent's model (Figure 3.2) does exactly that, by projecting the number of 20 year olds on a three year lag, minus the number of 63 year olds. This forecasts the net difference of those going to work and those retiring.

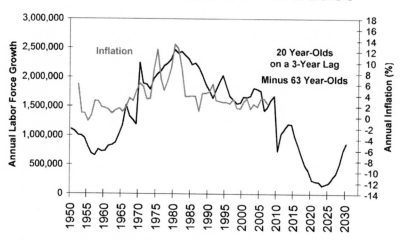

Source: HS Dent Foundation

Figure 3.2: Dent Inflation Forecast

This chart suggests that, due to the entry of the first wave of Echo Boomers (the children of the Baby Boomers) into the workforce, inflation should rise mildly through about 2009. After 2009, labor force growth actually goes negative, implying that inflation will grind to a halt. Naturally, this is not an exact measure. Baby Boomers could choose to work longer, which could postpone the workforce shrinkage. There could also be a shift in the percentage of women who choose to pursue gainful employment, which could shift the chart in either direction. Regardless, these changes would be marginal and the trend would remain the same. The main factor driving the deflationary forces after 2009 is not the retirement of the productive Boomers but rather a decrease in the workforce entry of their children. As we said earlier, young professionals are inflationary. Fewer young professionals mean less inflation.

But Isn't a Shrinking Workforce *Inflationary?*

The common view in academia is the demographic changes facing the country are inflationary. This view, explained most eloquently by Dr. Jeremy Siegel and Federal Reserve Chairman Ben Bernanke, can be summarized like this:

> As the Baby Boomers begin to retire, we will have comparatively fewer workers. This means that a smaller number of workers will have to work to support the consumption needs of the country. Fewer workers mean less production, or supply. If supply falls while demand remains the same, prices will have to rise as the marketplace reacts. Thus, we will have inflation. Furthermore, a shortage of labor could develop, which would force companies to raise wages in order to compete for workers, adding further inflationary pressure. The end result will be a form of 1970s-style stagflation, so the thinking goes.

While this view has its intuitive appeal, there are several flaws. We will attempt to debunk these flaws by using the example of a single extended family.

When a man and woman marry and begin to live together, they have certain economies of scale. Renting one apartment or making one mortgage payment is cheaper than two. Likewise, the couple shares one set of utility bills, furniture, linens, kitchen utensils, and every other facet of modern life.

When the couple begins to have children, life gets a lot more expensive. Suddenly, that small apartment needs to be bigger, as does the car. In addition to the regular expenses, the new parents can also add Junior's expenses for baby food and clothes, medical bills, and day care to the list. Things only get worse as Junior ages. Soon, the parents find themselves paying for swimming lessons, band camp, and college prep classes.

At this stage in his life, Junior is an inflationary pressure on the household. He produces nothing of economic value yet he consumes more and more, as all young adults do—on Mom and Dad's tab. Luckily for Mom and Dad's finances, Junior eventually moves out and gets a job. About this time, however, Grandma retires and decides to move into Junior's old room at Mom and Dad's house.

In the Siegel/Bernanke model, Grandma is considered to be every bit as inflationary as Junior, which assumes that children and the retired are interchangeable parts. Both consume and neither produce. Therefore, both are inflationary, right?

Wrong! Empirical evidence (and common sense) would tell us that a person's consumer spending is highly dependent on that person's age and stage of life. This is the foundation of the H.S. Dent Spending Wave, discussed in Chapter 1. A person can be expected to spend more every year of his or her life until their late 40s or early 50s today. With retirement in sight, people begin to consume less and save more. With the exception of healthcare, spending on virtually everything decreases in late career and retirement. Sure, Grandma has to eat, but she doesn't eat as much as a growing Junior, and Grandma isn't buying a new basketball hoop or the latest iPod. And she certainly isn't buying a new washer or dryer or big-screen plasma TV. It is the purchase of these big-ticket durable goods that boost aggregate demand and consumers peak in their demand for these items much earlier than retirement. This is the fundamental flaw in the Siegel/Bernanke argument. An aging population full of retirees spends substantially less money (especially on the highly leveraged durable goods) and is *de*flationary, not *in*flationary.

Siegel and Bernanke's view is contrary to the logic of the economic historians mentioned above, Fischer and Clark, and to the logic of the forecaster Harry Dent. All of the research described above makes a compelling point that falling (or aging) populations are deflationary. Yet the inflationary view persists and appears to be gaining acceptance. We will certainly find out soon enough which view is correct, as demographic changes are already underway.

This brings us back to good ol' Keynes and the demand side of the equation.

Turning Japanese

Lord Keynes wrote extensively about "excessive" savings and the "liquidity trap." In the Keynesian model, excessive savings are any savings in excess of those needed to fund investment. When investors perceive the returns on investments to be low, they simply save their money rather than invest it. They buy T-bills rather than build new factories or retail centers.

This creates a self-fulfilling prophesy of low returns and low investment known as the liquidity trap. Keynes pointed out that a fall in consumer spending or a decision by consumers to save a larger percentage of their incomes could be the cause of this vicious, deflationary cycle.

In turn, Harry Dent took the next step of identifying the root cause of that change in consumer behavior: age. The peaking of Dent's Spending Wave will very likely correspond to Keynes's dreaded combination of excessive savings and the liquidity trap. Luckily, for a real world example of the Keynesian nightmare scenario we have the experience of 1990s Japan.

Harry Dent first analyzed Japan's demographic trends in *The Great Boom Ahead*. For anyone who believes that Americans will never stop their "getting and spending," Figure 3.3 should be quite sobering. Japanese consumer spending has drifted downward since the late 1980s. The Japanese still live well, with lifestyles on par with those in the United States and Europe, but they spend less money than they used to. Not surprisingly, Japanese stocks have suffered over that time period, as the companies have faced their own liquidity traps. Why invest in new capacity if your domestic consumers are purchasing less every year?

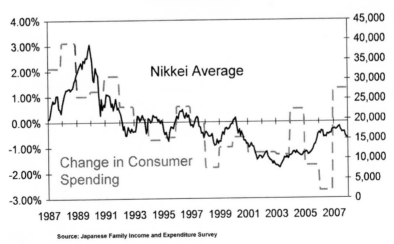

Japanese Stock Market vs. Change in Japanese Consumer Spending 1987 – 2007

Source: Japanese Family Income and Expenditure Survey

Figure 3.3: Japanese Change in Consumption and Stock Performance

We won't belabor the point here, as we've already described Japan's economic malaise in prior chapters. To summarize: Japan's population aged and began to spend less and save more, and when it did the economy stopped growing.

By Jeremy Siegel's analysis, Japan's population should be inflationary. Figure 3.4 takes a look at that population. With over 25% of the population over the age of 60, Japan should be downright *hyperinflationary*, on par with 1920s Weimer Republic Germany. But as seen in Figure 3.5, inflation has been virtually nonexistent since the early 1990s. In fact, the late 1990s and early 2000s witnessed mild *de*flation. If it weren't for the strong boom among Japan's major export partners, Japan would have likely experienced an even greater level of deflation.

Japan fell into the dreaded Keynesian liquidity trap due to its aging demographics. Following the standard Keynesian solution, the Japanese government initiated its infamous "Big Bang" in late 1996 in which the country went on the biggest public spending spree in its history. The belief was that a stimulative shock would shake Japan out of its liquidity trap and its habit of excess savings. Japan would become a "normal" country again economically.

You can see the effects of the Big Bang on Figure 3.5. There is a distinct blip in 1997 in which inflation crept up. The effects were short lived, however, and the CPI drifted lower for the next eight years. The Keynesian solution was clearly overpowered by Japan's demographic trends.

Japan Population

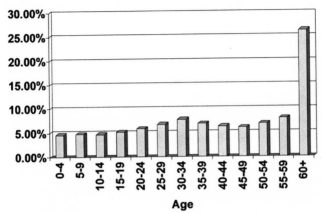

Source: United Nations

Figure 3.4: Japan Population

Japan Inflation
CPI in 2005 Yen

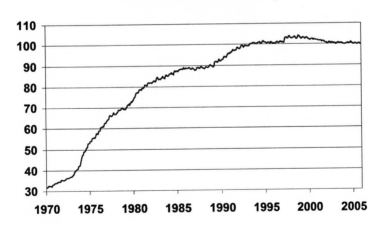

Source: Japan Statistics Bureau

Figure 3.5: Japan Inflation

Demographics are what led Japan into its liquidity trap, and demographics will be what lift Japan out of it, at least for a while. Courtesy of the HS Dent Foundation, Figure 3.6 is the Japan Spending Wave, defined here as the number of 45 to 49 year olds, or peak spenders. Japan's Spending Wave began to turn up in 2005 and will continue to do so until approximately 2020. This means that, despite an aging population, Japan should get some respite from its deflationary abyss. The Bank of Japan has cautiously stated that inflation has returned to Japan. We believe that Japan will enjoy the next 14 years or so with mild, tolerable inflation. After 2020, however, deflation and the dreaded liquidity trap should return with a vengeance. Unfortunately, there will be no demographic echo boom to save Japan the next time.

Japan Spending Wave

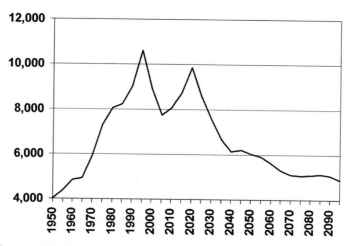

Source: HS Dent Foundation, from data provided by the United Nations

Figure 3.6: Japan Spending Wave

Deflation Isn't *All* Bad, Is It?

We have made the case that deflation, not inflation, will be the issue over the next 15 years or so as the massive Baby Boom generation in North America and Europe ages, begins to spend less, and then retires. Since these economies still dominate world GDP, they will likely cast a mild deflationary tone over the entire world economy until major emerging countries such as China and India are able to pick up the demand slack or until the West sees a resurgence in spending after 2020-2024.

As bad as deflation is, there are some residual benefits. Just as inflation is the economy's way of financing new generations and new innovations, deflation is the economy's way of "trimming the fat." In a deflationary environment of falling prices, weaker, less efficient companies and entire industries fail and are "shaken out." The strongest and best managed companies are the ones that survive and prosper in the process of creative destruction. Some of the America's finest companies were survivors of the Great Depression, such as General Electric. Even after enduring 16 years of semi-depression, Japan still boasts many world class companies. Toyota is widely considered to be the best car company in the world. The deflationary transformation in the United States will be unpleasant, but the end result will be a leaner, more efficient economy.

Already, there are certain industries for which deflation is a way of life. Consider semiconductors and computers. By the time Intel begins production on a new chip, there is already a newer, better one being designed that will make the existing chip obsolete. Prices in the industry are constantly falling, and only the strongest and most efficient companies are able to compete, which is why Intel has few competitors. Likewise, personal computers are constantly falling in price. The typical computer that a college freshman might take to his dorm has fallen from over $2,000 to less than $500, while the computational power has increased exponentially. Not surprisingly, the number of PC manufacturers is small and getting smaller every year.

As mentioned above, a concern expressed by both Jeremy Siegel and Ben Bernanke is that the mass retirement of the Baby Boomers will lead to a shortage of labor and that prices will have to rise as a result. But the truth is, the competitive, free-market economy has been making expensive human labor obsolete since the dawn of the Industrial Revolution. Barely 100 years ago, the United States was still largely an agrarian country. Today, less than 2% of the workforce works in agriculture, and the United States is the leading world producer of several staple crops. Due to productivity enhancements, American agriculture produces more than ever with less labor.

Similarly, manufacturing employment has been in decline in the United States since the 1970s. A fair amount of this is due to manufacturers moving their operations to China and other low-wage countries, but automation has "destroyed" more jobs through the decades than outsourcing or off-shoring and continues to do so today. Due to revolutions in computing and robotics systems, fewer workers are able to produce more goods and at a higher level of quality than ever before.

But what about services? The United States is a service economy, after all. You cannot build a computer or robot to do your taxes or cut your hair, can you?

Believe it or not, the answer is yes. Anyone who has experience with Turbo Tax knows that using a simple off-the-shelf software program is more than sufficient for doing all but the most complicated tax returns. As for hair cutting, just wait. We may never have robots that will cut your hair, but we already have robots and computer systems that perform any number of other tasks. Consider call centers. When was the last time you had to call American Airlines? You can now get any relevant flight information from a computerized system that understands your voice commands. Imagine the small fortune that the company has saved in salaries and benefits to would-be call center operators. The computerized voice on the other end of the line does not demand three weeks paid vacation or a generous pension, and will never go on strike. These savings allow American Airlines to keep its fares competitive, which is anti-inflationary.

Today, surgeons use robotic systems to assist with surgeries, but it is not just the high-value-added professions that utilize this technology. Even something as low-tech as a carwash no longer requires human attention. Think about that the next time you drive through an automated carwash and watch the robotic arms rub down your car.

Due to the implementation of Microsoft Office, most executives no longer need to employ a secretary. Most still employ assistants, but lower-end secretarial work has all but disappeared, replaced by application programs such as Word and Outlook. A person has been fully replaced by lines of software code, code that can be reproduced an infinite number of times by Microsoft at a marginal cost of *zero*.

The same may eventually be true of waiters and waitresses. Decades ago, McDonalds started the fast food trend in which a small number of low-skilled workers could produce a massive quantity of food. Today, even mid-priced restaurants are following this model. The popular Asian chain Pei Wei operates with a very small staff of food runners— no full service waiters or waitresses needed.

The drive through operator in fast food restaurants is no longer needed either. The oil-producing parts of Montana are booming, and the McDonalds in the area are not able to find enough low-skilled labor to keep their drive-through window staffed. Cheap information technology enables this job to be outsourced: to India, Nebraska, or the moon, for that matter. It may be just a matter of time until McDonald's uses the American Airlines computerized voice to take your order.

It doesn't stop there. Robots could soon be a cost-effective way to avoid paying a maid or gardener. Already, the iRobot Roomba 560 is an automated robotic vacuum cleaner that cleans your floor while you're at work. The Roomba has a self-adjusting floor sensor that enables it to seamlessly glide over all of the various surfaces in your home: carpet, wood, tile…even *shag* carpet, if you're in to that sort of thing. Meanwhile, Belrobotics is rapidly developing robotic lawnmowers that can safely and cheaper cut your grass while you spent your Saturday drinking lemonade by the pool.

Even the ancient profession of soldiering is using robots to replace people. The recent wars in Afghanistan and Iraq demonstrated America's new prowess at using unmanned "drones" to do reconnaissance. Other robots search for bombs or explore enemy trenches. And for even more examples of the future of labor, we need only look east. In Japan, some companies have experimented with using robots as receptionists and security guards. Even police work can be partially replaced by machines. Digital cameras keep a watchful eye over most of London, reducing the need for beat cops patrolling the streets. Some police work in the United States is even done by "volunteers." Though some may criticize them as vigilantes, the Minutemen civilian militia that patrols the U.S./Mexico border may well be the wave of the future. Cash-strapped governments could conceivably "outsource" the work of policing to civilian groups who work in tandem with professional law enforcement. This may not be desirable (it may, in fact, even be quasi-anarchy), but technology combined with public cooperation could be seen as preferable to higher taxes to pay for the salaries and benefits of professional security. Only time will tell.

We should stop here before this chapter begins to resemble the Jetsons cartoon. We are not utopians forecasting a time where robots quietly work while humans live a life of luxury rivaling that of an Egyptian pharaoh. Our point is simply that advances in technology make any prolonged labor shortage extremely unlikely. Rising wages give more incentive to innovate and introduce labor-saving technologies. This is *de*flationary, not *in*flationary.

Inflate and Innovate!

Inflation occurs in periods when the population is expanding rapidly and thus consuming more. With the existing technologies and levels of productivity, supply is not able to meet demand, and the result is inflation. But this kind of inflation is self-correcting in the industrial and post-industrial eras, as entrepreneurs invent and use new technologies to delivery the goods and lower the cost. So, inflation coincides with and leads to innovation, which in turn eliminates inflation. This has been true of every major innovation since before the cotton gin, and it will continue to be true going forward.

In this sense, *natural* inflation is a blessing, as it spurs the new technologies and business practices that eventually help to destroy it. This is exactly what we witnessed in the 1980s and 1990s, as the Baby Boomers became productive users of new technologies in their jobs and inflation rates fell as a result. Of course, artificial *monetary* inflation of the kind described by Milton Friedman and Ben Bernanke distorts this process and limits its effectiveness, but even this less desirable form of inflation has its small residual benefits. As a way of coping with Brazil's long history of hyperinflation, Brazilian banks have developed into some of the savviest users of technology in the world. Brazilian banks are far more efficient than most of their American or European counterparts in clearing checks and making funds available for use.

Once inflation subsides, as it has in Brazil, the innovations put in place remain, adding to future productivity.

Technology Cannot Save Us From the Liquidity Trap

To repeat, supply will not be an inflationary issue going forward. The capitalist system will generally find a way to deliver the goods and services. In fact, strong productivity in the West from new technologies and increased production from emerging powers like China and India are likely to create *excess* supply.

What capitalism will not do is guarantee that someone will actually *buy* the goods and services delivered. While a robot may be able to vacuum your carpet, it won't be buying a new pair of Gap jeans or a weekend at Disney World. The challenge going forward will be a lack of consumer demand, and thus deflation. This means that individuals and businesses will be well advised to prepare by trimming back their debts and becoming more financially conservative.

One final note is in order. Although the trends in place are clearly deflationary, we may never see actually true deflation. As both Milton Friedman and "Helicopter Ben" Bernanke have stressed, the Fed does have the ability to "print money" via open market operations and lowering interest rates. In Japan, interest rates dropped to 0%, and every monetary and fiscal stimulus known to mankind was employed. The Japanese ended up with flat prices and only sporadic and mild deflation. They also found themselves with a weak currency and with a dangerous level of government debt equal 170% of GDP (compared to 65% in the United States in 2008). This proves that there is no Keynesian "fix" to the demographic challenges we face going forward.

Chapter 4: International Prospects

We have established the direction that the U.S. economy is likely to go in the coming years due to the aging of the population. It won't be pretty. But what of the rest of the world? Western Europe's prospects look very similar to those of the United States. Australia's are slightly better, though certainly not great. By and large, the entire developed world faces rather difficult prospects. How about China and India? Might these two emerging giants continue their meteoric rises?

The following sections take a look at the potential to foreign markets with a special emphasis on China and India. In the coming decades, the world economy will be driven by Asia to a degree not seen in hundreds of years. But don't get too excited just yet: China too will be plagued by negative demographic trends just a few short years after the West. It will be India that emerges as the next major economic power, but even this is contingent on peace with its neighbors and the uplifting of its large population into a middle-class society. One thing is certain, however. The world economy will look much, much different in the coming decades.

The Paradox of China

"Jobs Lost as Manufacturing Shifts to China"

The generic headline printed above could have appeared in any American or European newspaper. It seems that no other country has generated both the desperate fear and the wild-eyed optimism that China has over the past decade. The same American or European that lives in dread of losing his job to a lower-wage Chinese worker also dreams of getting rich by investing in the explosive growth of the country. Thus the paradox of China in the minds of Westerners.

The paradox of China goes much deeper, however. China is one of the primary engines of the global economy. The recent boom in commodities has been driven largely by China's insatiable thirst for raw materials to feed their manufacturing juggernaut and build the necessary infrastructure. China is also becoming the hub of an expanding Asian economic bloc, gradually assuming the role that Japan has played for the past several decades. The Chinese economy has posted growth rates that are almost unbelievably high and largely without much of the inflation that has derailed many of the would-be developing-world success stories over the past fifty years.

At the same time, China's success comes at a price. China has, by most accounts, become an ecological disaster. This is likely to get much worse before it gets better, as China has been opening a major new coal plant every two weeks on average. And as the country has grown wealthier, the number of cars and trucks on the road has grown exponentially, along with the accompanying tailpipe exhaust.

Furthermore, the country's success may be extremely fragile, as it rests on several imbalances. China's age demographics are the most wildly out of proportion of any major country, as are China's gender demographics. As a result, its economy is likely to peak and slow much sooner than most economists expect. Another issue is China's government which, for any of its faults, has provided stability. Middle-class societies generally demand more democratic and accountable government. If China's rulers relax the grip that they have held on the country's political development for the past fifty years, the country could become less stable for a period. Finally, China's enormous wealth has come largely from exports and capital spending, not domestic consumption. This makes China particularly susceptible to downturns in the economies of its trading partners—such as the long-term decline we forecast for the United States and Europe starting around the end of this decade. So, while China's growth is truly commendable, we see it as being rather tenuous.

A Great Leap Forward into Capitalism

To get an idea of how truly impressive China's growth has been, we take a look at Figure 4.1. This chart indexes China's real GDP to its 1952 value. We should repeat that this is *real GDP*, not nominal, meaning that China's growth is legitimate and not merely the result of inflation or manipulated monetary policy. GDP growth has clearly been exponential, not linear, and as a result the detail of the early years is obscured. For this reason, a log scale is more appropriate (Figure 4.2).

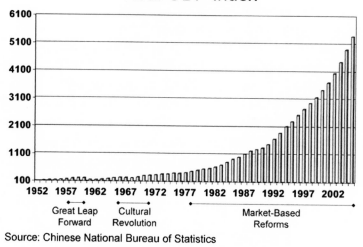

Figure 4.1: Chinese GDP Growth

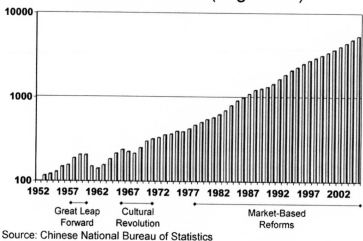

Figure 4.2: Chinese GDP Growth (Log Scale)

In Figure 4.2, we get a better representation of Chinese growth over the past half century. The 1950s and 1960s was a rough ride for the Chinese economy. Mao Zedong's ideological purges led to an enormous contraction in GDP and the destruction of the livelihood of virtually the entire population. In fact, the contraction was probably much worse than represented in this chart, as economic stats from the Mao era are notoriously unreliable and inflated.

Starting in 1978, the chart begins to rise dramatically due to the economic liberalizations of Deng Xiaoping. For the first time since the founding of the communist regime, foreign investment and limited private ownership began to take root. From that point on, China's growth has been virtually non-stop, and the country has firmly entrenched itself in the global financial system.

Among major Western countries, the United States has enjoyed the highest growth rates in recent years. Since 1980, real growth in U.S. GDP has averaged just under 3% per year. To keep things in perspective, over the same time period China's real GDP has grown at 9.5%—*more than three times the American rate.*

So, even though China started from a much lower base, the country is rapidly catching up to the West. Figure 4.3 compares Chinese and Western European per capita GDP, which is a better measure of true progress for the average citizen. By this chart, China's growth is even more impressive. The gains that took Western Europe centuries have taken the Chinese two and a half decades. Were these trends to continue much longer, China could match and overtake the West in GDP per capita by 2050.

GDP per Capita in China vs. Western Europe
400-1998

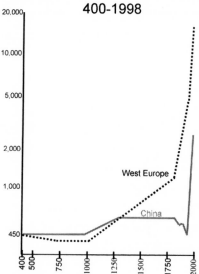

Source: *The World Economy:A Millennial Perspective, pg 42*

Figure 4.3: GDP Per Capita in China vs. Western Europe

To facilitate this incredible growth, the Chinese have built untold thousands of miles of world-class new roads, and the major Chinese cities now have skylines that rival New York or Chicago. China appears to be an unstoppable machine. The "China story" has so much appeal that it inspired veteran investor Jim Rogers, the legendary *Investment Biker* and business partner of George Soros, to actually pick up his family and move there to take advantage of the opportunities. (Mr. Rogers subsequently changed his mind due to the poor air quality and moved instead to Singapore.)

Rogers is certainly not the only Western investor looking to increase his fortunes in China. Foreign direct investment has been pouring into the country at a torrid pace for years. A.T. Kearney ranked China at the top of its Foreign Direct Investment ("FDI") Confidence Index (Figure 4.4), and the country has a healthy lead over its emerging market rival India and over traditional FDI destinations like the United States and United Kingdom. Clearly, international businesses continue to see excellent opportunities in China.

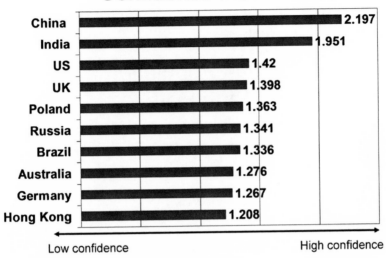

Figure 4.4: Foreign Direct Investment Confidence Index

While China's recent success has justified much of this optimism, we do believe that the end of the boom will come much sooner than most investors realize.

The Chinese Spending Wave

China's demographics are unique among developing countries. In the normal development of a country, birthrates fall gradually as urbanization increases. In other words, as people move from the country to the city—and thus leave the traditional, agrarian way of life for the early stages of an urban consumer lifestyle—they have fewer children. In a densely populated city or even suburb, it is simply not economical to have a large family.

We can use the United States as an example (Figure 4.5). By 1950, the United States had already long undergone its great migration from the farms to the cities, and a large majority of the population was urbanized. The new massive migration to the suburbs first caused births to increase, as did the return of soldiers from World War II.

But from a longer-term perspective, the number of children born per woman had already fallen to less than four and has since drifted lower, hovering near two since 1975. This is what a modern, urban society looks like, and this is the path that most populations take due to natural economic and lifestyle incentives.

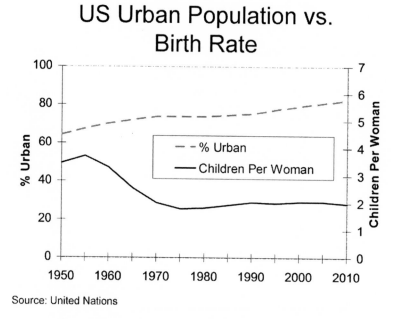

Source: United Nations

Figure 4.5: U.S. Urban Population vs. Birth Rates

China, in contrast, is a case study in everything that can go wrong in a planned economy. Mao Zedong encouraged the Chinese to have large families, while at the same time his policies stifled the economy. The result was a poor and overpopulated country in which a shrinking pool of wealth had to be distributed over an increasingly large population—a serious imbalance and the worst possible scenario.

The imbalance doesn't stop there, however. The Chinese government dramatically changed its course in the early 1970s and went so far as to institute the infamous One Child Policy in 1979, which remains in effect today. Interestingly, Figure 4.6 illustrates that the plunge in Chinese births began before these measures were taken, no doubt in response to the social and economic turmoil of late 1960s China. From the mid 1970s onward, the progressive rise in urbanization would have reduced birth rates to a fair extent even without the One Child Policy.

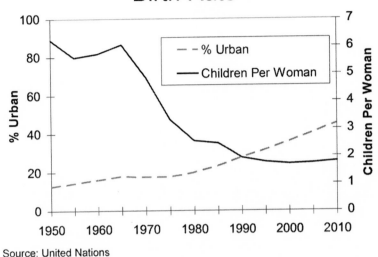

Source: United Nations

Figure 4.6: Chinese Urban Population vs. Birthrate

The end result is that China's births have plunged to the level of a developed Western country even though over half the population remains non-urbanized. China's birth rate per woman is 1.8 vs. 2.0 in the US, and as we will show ahead, China will see increasingly fewer women in the future as male babies are favored.

While China's economy continues to boom, the Chinese population—like the populations of the West—is now aging at an alarming rate. Urbanization will continue as young people flock to the cities, but the countryside will soon begin to resemble an enormous nursing home, as it will be populated primarily by the elderly.

The West has accumulated enough wealth to at least somewhat manage the economic consequences of its aging populations. Growth and living standards in the West will likely stagnate in coming decades, but at least Westerners have already achieved a high standard of living. China's predicament is much worse. To borrow a phrase from demographer Phillip Longman, "it appears that China will grow old before it grows rich."

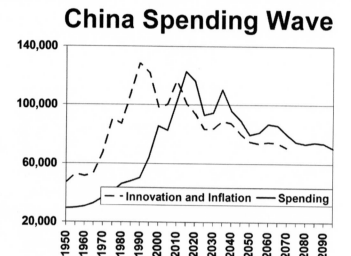

China Spending Wave

Source: HS Dent Foundation, from data provided by the United Nations

Figure 4.7: China Spending Wave

We can glean several important pieces of insight from China's Spending and Innovation Waves Figure 4.7, courtesy of the H.S. Dent Foundation. (For a detailed explanation of the Dent Spending Wave methodology, see Chapter 1.[8])

China's Innovation Wave already peaked in 1990, and its smaller, secondary peak should hit around 2010. While the boom in foreign direct investment might be able to compensate to an extent for declining domestic innovation, the trend is clearly down after 2010. There is another key point here that should be mentioned. The Innovation Wave tracks 20-24-year-olds over time. The peak ages for migration are in the 25-29 year range. So, by pushing the Innovation Wave forward by five years, you should be able to get an estimate of when China's urbanization rate should begin to slow. China should hit its secondary migration peak around 2015—less than a decade from now.

---

8   For a longer explanation of the Spending Wave / Innovation Wave methodology as applied to China and other countries of the world, we recommend *Changing Global Demographics*, an HS Dent special report available on www.hsdent.com and in major online bookstores.

Without a steady flow of young migrants from the country, the growth of China's cities will slow. China would also lose the chief source of its cheap labor—a seemingly inexhaustible supply of young Chinese men and women willing and able to work for low wages. Productivity enhancements can alleviate this to an extent, but the fact remains that China will not maintain one of the key advantages it has enjoyed up to this point.

2015 also represents another, even greater turning point. China's Spending Wave peaks in that year as well. Today, due in large part to the wealth being generated by China's booming export economy, a Chinese middle class is rapidly developing. As HS Dent has explained for years, it is the middle class "keeping up with the Joneses" that makes a domestic economy stable and predictable. Unfortunately for China, the Chinese Spending Wave will peak before this middle class fully develops, effectively nipping it in the bud. It appears that China really may grow old before it grows rich. The country may never reach the levels of urbanization and standard of living of the West, or if it does, it will probably take much longer than most commentators assume.

Can China Export its Way to Prosperity?

A common argument is that China can continue to prosper due to high exports. We see several flaws with this argument. To start, no country's advantages last forever. The other developing Asian counties will find ways to compete with their colossal neighbor in the coming years. And even if China were capable of maintaining its export dominance indefinitely, the disadvantage to such a position is that it makes its economy more susceptible to changes in the world economy. In 2008, China followed the United States and Europe into a significant economic slowdown that may just be starting. Japan had sizable trade surpluses throughout the 1990s, yet the country remained mired in a grinding, 16-year, slow-motion depression. That was due to its domestic downturn in consumption that is similar to what we see coming on a much larger scale in the West. Japan's downturn was partially mitigated by its exports, but in the global environment that we forecast, China's boom will be derailed by its export exposure.

Japan has been long feared by its competitors as an exporting powerhouse, but when compared to China on a percent of GDP basis, Japan's exports are minimal. Figure 4.8 ranks China, Japan, the United States, and India by exports as a percentage of GDP. Exports make up a third of Chinese GDP, compared to just 12% in Japan. China's economy may very well be the most unbalanced of any major country in history. Any sustained slowing in exports will send ripples through the Chinese economy.

Exports and GDP

Country	GDP ($US)	Exports ($US)	Exports as a % of GDP
China	2,224,811,000,000	752,200,000,000	33.8%
Japan	4,571,314,000,000	550,500,000,000	12.0%
India	775,410,000,000	76,230,000,000	9.8%
United States	12,485,725,000,000	927,500,000,000	7.4%

Source: IMF, CIA Word Factbook

Figure 4.8: Exports and GDP

Japan's exports were not able to lift the country out of it 1990s recession, despite the fact that virtually the entire rest of the world was booming. China will not have that benefit. Its domestic economy continues to point up into 2015, but what will happen after that point, when it naturally begins to slow and while the rest of the world is slowing as well?

Using the Dent demographic forecasting model, the major economies of the West should be in a slow decline for years to come. China's trade with neighboring Asian countries will be less affected, but the net result should still be a noticeable slowing in China's export growth. China will need to look to its domestic market for demand; the problem is, domestic demand should be stalling just five years later in 2015. Increasing trade to growing areas like Southeast Asia and India will be key for stemming the falling tide of exports to the West.

While we don't see China reverting to Mao-era levels of poverty and deprivation, we do believe that China's growth and influence in the global economy will be substantially curtailed after 2015, and the Chinese economy will likely suffer through a fair amount of turmoil as its imbalances are sorted out.

In the short-term, is China doomed due to its export exposure? The country's stock market performance during the volatile months of late 2007 and 2008 could be an early indication. The World Bank offers some insightful comments in its February 2008 *China Quarterly Update*. The Bank reports,

> China's economy has begun to slow down somewhat from its record growth rates earlier in 2007. The domestic economy has started to contribute more to growth, and the trade surplus may stop rising going forward. Food prices lifted headline inflation to 6.5 in December, but general inflation pressure (except food) remains modest....
>
> **The slowdown in demand was due to a declining contribution of external trade [i.e. net exports] to GDP growth, partly offset by a rising contribution of domestic demand.** Export growth had started to outpace import growth by a large margin in early 2006. Since then, a substantial share of GDP growth was due to net trade. However, in the second half of 2007, import growth picked up while export growth declined and imports outpaced exports for 3 consecutive months in the fourth quarter. As a result, the contribution of net trade to growth came down, particularly in the fourth quarter. Most of the impact on overall GDP growth was offset by an apparent rebound in domestic demand growth....

While China's stock market fell hard during the credit crunch—along with those of virtually every other country in the world—China's domestic economy appears to be humming right along. If the past year is any indication, China's growth in GDP is gradually becoming less dependent on exports and more dependent on domestic consumption, which is good for long-term stability. If true, this would make China's economy far more stable and predictable than it is today. We remain skeptical of these finding for reasons to be discussed, but for now we will continue with the World Bank analysis. Figure 4.9 is compiled from the World Bank's China GDP data.

China Growth Rates

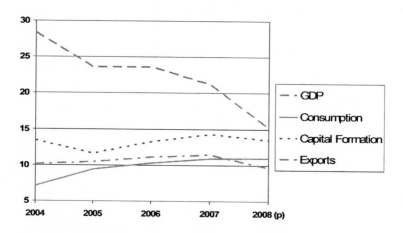

Source: World Bank China Quarterly Update, February 2008

Figure 4.9: China Growth Rates

China's torrid GDP growth rate has hovered around 10% for the past several years, though it is projected to decline slightly in 2008. As the World Bank notes, Chinese consumer spending growth continues to accelerate and is projected to grow faster than the overall GDP in 2008. The growth rate in exports has been falling, though still remains considerably higher than all other GDP components.

It is important to draw the right conclusions from this chart. **Chinese exports are not falling**, but their rate of growth is indeed slowing. Exports are still growing at an almost absurdly high 15-20% per year, numbers that would make virtually any other country on earth green with envy. Only in a country that had growth rates in excess of 25% could a rate of "only" 15% seem disappointing. These downward trends should continue if only for the reason that 25% year-over-year growth rates are simply not sustainable over time. If those rates continued to compound at 25%, China's exports alone would be larger than today's total *world* GDP in less than 20 years, and this is obviously an impossibility. China's export growth, though still high, will continue to slow to a more long-term feasible rate.

The Capital Spending Juggernaut

Of course, China's export bubble would not be possible without the accompanying bubble in capital spending. You can't export widgets, after all, unless you first build a widget factory and the necessary transportation infrastructure to bring those widgets to market. In fact, by some measures, it is the investment boom that is the real China story, and that exports, when calculated properly, are a far more manageable chunk of the Chinese economy than our number would suggest. The *Economist* writes,

> The headline ratio of exports to GDP is very misleading. It compares apples and oranges: exports are measured as gross revenue while GDP is measured in value-added terms. Jonathan Anderson, an economist at UBS, a bank, has tried to estimate exports in value-added terms by stripping out imported components, and then converting the remaining domestic content into value-added terms by subtracting inputs purchased from other domestic sectors....
>
> Once these adjustments are made, Mr. Anderson reckons that the "true" export share is just under 10% of GDP. That makes China slightly more exposed to exports than Japan, but nowhere near as export-led as Taiwan or Singapore.... Indeed, China's economic performance during the global IT slump in 2001 showed that a collapse in exports is not the end of the world. The annual rate of growth in its exports fell by a massive 35 percentage points from peak to trough during 2000-01, yet China's overall GDP growth slowed by less than one percentage point. Employment figures also confirm that exports' share of the economy is relatively small. Surveys suggest that one-third of manufacturing workers are in export-oriented sectors, which is equivalent to only 6% of the total workforce.[9]

---

9   Except from "An Old Chinese Myth," *The Economist*. January 5, 2008

We find this analysis to be interesting, but we also take it with the proverbial grain of salt. Given the Chinese government's reputation and lack of transparency, any and all of China's economic statistics should be viewed with extreme suspicion. No matter how you slice the numbers, exports are still an incredible source of growth for China's economy. Exports are largely what have provided the hard currency with which to purchase imports and have provided much of the business justification for China's massive foreign direct investment. China is a booming example of Say's Law in action. Supply has created its own demand; China's export economy has given wages to its workers and profits to its capitalists and has in turn created a massive demand for both raw materials and finished products from abroad. Under its old Maoist economy, there was no consumer demand because there were no consumers, only peasants living a subsistence lifestyle. Today, China has a vibrant middle class with a standard of living to defend. But at less than 40% of GDP by most credible measures, we are not yet convinced that China's consumer spending is big enough to carry the economic torch. It may eventually, but in the meantime China is still highly dependent on exports and capital spending to keep its economic engine running.

In the same article, the *Economist* mentions that capital spending accounts for 40% of the Chinese economy, significantly larger than exports, no matter how they are measured. Even if most of this investment is used to satisfy domestic consumption (the *Economist* suggests that only 14% of the investment is dependent on exports), an economy dependent on capital spending is a bubble economy prone to massive and disruptive booms and busts. The 1990s tech boom and bust in the United States is a fine example, as are the canal and railroad booms of prior centuries.

Investment booms and busts are not all bad, of course. The overcapacity in IT infrastructure in the 1990s led to a massive reduction in communications costs and made new innovations like internet telephony possible. Though the investors that funded the infrastructure boom lost billions in the shakeout of 2000-2002, the world economy continues to benefit today from the productivity boost that the cheap information technology made possible.

It is also far from certain how "excessive" some of China's headline investment is. China's roads were in bad condition just a few short years ago; wouldn't the massive investment in new roads be justified? A separate *Economist* article recounts that, at nearly two miles in length, the newest terminal in Beijing's airport is bigger than the entirety London's Heathrow airport, the busiest airport in the world. But shouldn't a country as large as China have an appropriately large airport for its massive capital city? The Beijing airport is already the ninth busiest in the world, and climbing. The same article outlines the full extent of China's infrastructure boom: $200 billion in rail projects, bridges that break world records for length, 70,000 kilometers of new highways.... The scale is mind-boggling. But, as with the tech boom of the 1990s, much of it is justified and sorely needed. There are plenty of anecdotal stories of Alaska-style "bridges to nowhere," but how big are these projects relative to the total? The truth is, no one knows, and typically it doesn't become known until *after* the subsequent bust.

So what does this mean for China? Is a bust imminent? Unfortunately, all bubbles have to eventually burst, and the combination of rising domestic inflation pressures and then a global slowdown lead by North America and Europe would provide the perfect environment for China's stock and economic bubble to burst in the next few years.

China will very likely suffer an enormous deflationary "shake out" and bust at some point in the relatively near future, but when? What will be the proverbial straw that breaks the camel's back? Will it be more rising oil and commodity prices or a continued and more dramatic weakening of the U.S. economy and a subsequent stalling in export growth? Or what about an ecological disaster that prompts stricter environmental regulation? If history is any guide, China will suffer a major bust, just as most other emerging markets did in 1998 and just as the United States did early in its industrial development. Our best estimate is that it will happen along the same timeline as the bust in the US, between 2009 and 2011. The question then becomes, what happens after the bust? Following the Chinese Spending Wave, we believe that China will recover after a bust, even if it proves to be a deep and destabilizing one. The forces at work are simply too powerful to be stopped...yet.

This does not mean that China equity investors will not suffer in the meantime. The recent credit crisis that started in the American subprime mortgage market quickly spread across the globe, proving yet again that emerging markets are far from insulated from downturns in America and the rest of the developed world. As the market action of late 2007 and 2008 has shown, even if China's economy is starting to mildly decouple from the West, its stock market certainly has not. During times of crisis, investors become more risk averse and punish nearly all speculative sectors. This is an important point to remember.

The J Curve

China has another major imbalance with which to contend: the paradox of creating a liberated economy while maintaining an authoritarian, non-democratic government. In England and later the United States, political liberties accelerated with the emergence of the middle classes. English landed nobles began to chip away at the edifice of the authoritarian state when they forced the King to sign the Magna Carta in 1215. This was not as clean as the modern history student imagines; King John fought this concession tooth and nail, and the country nearly fell into full-scale civil war.

Since that time, the march has been toward greater liberty, but again, the process was never clean. Today, the "people" rule England through Parliament. But getting to this stage required a bloody civil war in the mid-1600s, an Oliver Cromwell dictatorship, the Glorious Revolution of William and Mary, the English Bill of Rights, and innumerable other power struggles on a smaller scale. The United States inherited these nascent democratic ideals and took them a step further in the American Revolution of the late 1700s. But even the United States did not become fully democratic in the modern sense until the women's suffrage movement of the early 1900s and the abolition of the Jim Crow laws in the 1950s.

Today, the United States is the most politically stable country in the world. Even the disputed presidential election of 2000 was a minor event, as there was never any legitimate fear of civil war as a result. Our threats come from the outside—from terrorism and etc.—from being the leading country in the world and the biggest target.

After the English blazed the trail of modern freedom and democracy, the timeline has been much shorter for each subsequent country to undergo the process. Still, no country has made the transaction completely "cleanly." Much of Latin America and the former Soviet Union are still struggling with the process today, while China has yet to really begin.

This brings us to an interesting piece of recent scholarship by Ian Bremmer. In attempting to explain the relationship between stability and freedom, the political scientist created the J Curve. To summarize Bremmer's work, a country can achieve stability by being free and stable—like the United States or United Kingdom—but a country can also achieve it by being oppressive and totalitarian—like China or the authoritarian governments of the Middle East.

An example might be modern Iraq. The Saddam Hussein dictatorship was ruthless, but stable. A democratic Iraq, if it can ever be created, could eventually be stable as well, once the appropriate institutions were created and solidified. The problem is that the transition period is extremely unstable, as we see today.

Figure 4.10 illustrates the J-Curve, with our own rough estimates for the placement of the US, China, India and Iraq along the curve. We are not suggesting that China will ever descend into the level of anarchy that Iraq finds itself in today; clearly every country has its own unique circumstances. But the point is clear: in order for China to become a free society, the country will have to suffer some amount of instability in the intermediate term. As China's citizens grow wealthier in the next few years, there will be increasing calls for expanded freedoms, and in fact, there already have been. This is unquestionably a good thing, but it is likely to cause many a Western investor to lose sleep in the interim.

On the other hand, major revolutions tend to come from large, young generations that are idealistic and change-oriented. Given that China is aging rapidly due to its One Child Policy and large-scale urbanization since 1979, China does not have such a rebellious young generation. The Innovation Wave in Figure 4.7 peaked in 1990—just a year after the 1989 Tiananmen Square protest that was brutally squashed. The echo baby boom in China peaks in its Innovation Wave by 2010. So going forward, the capacity for a sustained revolution from a young, rising middle class will increasingly fade. China may simply move incrementally towards more freedom and reforms within a one party system that is top-down in its political control without ever developing Western-style parliamentary democracy. Something akin to 1970s Spain in the later, softer stages of the Franco regime might be a good historical precedent. Only unlike Spain, there is no restless young generation to push for an eventual revolutionary change.

The J Curve
Government Stability vs. Openness

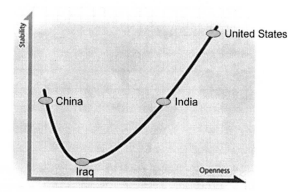

Source: *The J Curve: A New Way to Understand Why Nations Rise and Fall*
(Chinese, American, Indian, and Iraqi estimates by Sizemore and Robinson)

Figure 4.10: The J-Curve

A 30-Million Man Problem

On a side note, China has one other complication from its One Child policy that has created yet another imbalance. When limited to only one child, most Chinese couples prefer a boy. The result has been an enormous surge in the abortion of females, and the largest gender imbalance in history.

Nature produces slightly more women than men, and male deaths in wars and longer female life expectancy have always tended to produce societies with more women than men. Yet due to the selective abortions of female fetuses, the numbers in China have been almost incredibly skewed in the opposite direction. In 2005, male births outnumbered female by a ration of 118 to 100. By 2020, it is estimated that there will be 30 million more men than women in the 20-45-year age group. This means 30 million men with no prospects for marriage or the civilizing behavior that stable married life helps to create. We would expect prostitution and the other social ills that tend to accompany it, such as drug and alcohol abuse and gambling, to be a real concern going forward. It is also worth noting that, since it is women who conceive and have babies, the mass abortion of female fetuses has wiped out a significant number of future would-be mothers. When China's population begins to contract around 2035, those would-be mothers and their would-be children will be sorely missed.

Alternatives to China

China is a country with great opportunities but also major problems. The country has an age and gender demographic imbalance that is arguably an existential threat, an economy that is skewed heavily on exports to regions that are set to decline, an environment that is rapidly being destroyed by nonexistent regulation, and a political establishment that is in major need of reform. With these in mind, China might best be avoided for companies and investors that are not already successfully established there.

We would recommend India as an alternative. India has lagged China in its development, but the country is making steady progress. Unlike China, which has built a world-class manufacturing and export economy, India has skipped that stage and moved directly to an emerging services and information based economy. India's growing and well-educated middle class puts the country in perfect position to take advantage of Thomas Friedman's "flat world" of globalization. Furthermore, should countries start to put up barriers to trade (as we have already seen in the United States and Europe in the collapse of the Doha Round, the nixing of the Dubai Ports deal, and numerous attempts by European companies to block mergers), China's physical exports will be much easier targets than India's intangible services and information.

As seen in Figure 4.8, India's economy is far less reliant on exports. India's domestic market is the focus of its economy, and this is good news. India, unlike China, has no expected peak in its Spending Wave for many decades to come. India will suffer far less than China from the downturn in the West.

Furthermore, India has already made it through the difficult part of the J Curve. We estimate India's stability as being roughly equal to China's, but on the "right" side of the curve. India is a parliamentary democracy and enjoys personal liberties and, for the most part, the rule of law.

India is not without its own problems, however. Though democratic, its government has traditionally been hostile to capitalism. It is also unnecessarily bureaucratic, and the state wastes far too many resources that could be better spent in the private sector by India's world-class entrepreneurs and professionals or even by a more effective government. India roads and schools are in terrible condition, and most of the country's infrastructure is in need of expansion or replacement.

On balance, India's prospects look far better than those of their large neighbor to the east. India is starting to recognize that it needs to create more domestic capital and to attract more foreign direct investment to create the modern infrastructure needed to leverage its massive underemployed labor pool. This will take time—but India has time. Figure 4.11, courtesy of the HS Dent Foundation, shows how India's Innovation Wave will rise dramatically into 2040 and its Spending Wave doesn't peak until around 2065.

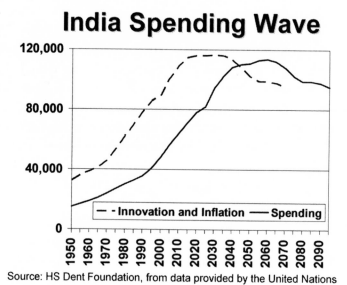

Source: HS Dent Foundation, from data provided by the United Nations

Figure 4.11: India Spending Wave

India will have a golden opportunity in the years to come to establish a new leadership role in the world economy through economic reforms and growth in foreign direct investment, and it should prove nearly immune to the global downturn due to its low export exposure.

Chapter 5: International Prospects, Part II

The Riches of India

Chances are good that you have found yourself in the following situation: You call your phone company or credit card bank to ask a question about your bill, and your call is taken by a friendly man with a distinct accent named "John."

After some short pleasantries, John walks you through your bill step-by-step—from a call center halfway across the world in India.

Coupled with the trend in globalization, the communications technology revolution of the 1990s has transformed an impoverished, Soviet-inspired state into a booming center of world capitalism in which entrepreneurs like Bill Gates are greeted with more pomp and circumstance than most visiting heads of state. Despite the economic reforms of the past two decades, India's state sector is still in drastic need of reform. Perhaps even worse, most of India's roads are in abysmal repair, and the traffic congestion in most cities is a major drain on productivity. Moreover, large segments of India's population remain in abject poverty. The *Financial Times* reports that there is one toilet for every 1,500 people in some of the poorer parts of Mumbai (previously known as Bombay).

The good news is that the power of information technology has allowed the new economy to largely bypass many of these problems altogether. It has also brought unprecedented wealth to India's educated middle class while supplying the West with a vast supply of skilled knowledge workers at a fraction of the price it would cost at home.

This new generation of young professionals is earning and spending at an unprecedented rate for India, and this trend will only continue as they progress through their life cycles—marrying, buying homes, and raising their children—spending ever more in the "keeping up with the Joneses" tradition of Middle America. Even though the country is still in the early stages of its economic modernization, over the longer term India's prospects are brighter than those of China, South Korea and Taiwan. In the July/August 2006 edition of *Foreign Affairs*, Gurcharan Das published an insightful article titled "The India Model" that explains how the country has taken a very different path from most of its contemporaries in Asia. It is one particular development—the emergence of a viable domestic consumer economy—that we find particularly appealing:

> In the past two decades, the size of the middle class has quadrupled (to almost 250 million people)…At the same time, population growth has slowed from the historic rate of 2.2 percent a year to 1.7 percent today—meaning that growth has brought large per capita income gains, from $1,178 to $3,051 (in terms of purchasing-power parity) since 1980. India is now the world's fourth-largest economy. Soon it will surpass Japan to become the third-largest [as measured by purchasing-power parity].

> The notable thing about India's rise is not that it is new, but that its path has been unique. Rather than adopting the classic Asian strategy—exporting labor-intensive, low-priced manufactured goods to the West—*India has relied on its domestic market more than exports, consumption more than investment, services more than industry, and high-tech more than low-skilled manufacturing* [Emphasis ours]. This approach has meant that the Indian economy has been mostly insulated from global downturns, showing a degree of stability that is as impressive as the rate of its expansion.

This is a crucial point; with most of the developed world facing the potential for an unprecedented demographic-induced recession or even depression, countries that have viable domestic consumer markets should fare much better than those that are focused on exporting to the West. This makes India's growth boom much more durable than that of, say, China. Das's article points out that personal consumption accounts for 64% of India's economy, compared to 58 percent for Europe, 55 percent for Japan, and 42 percent for China. As we have noted, U.S. consumption has hovered around the 70% mark for many years, proving that a country can grow and prosper with a consumption-driven economy. In an economy dominated by services and information—like that of the United States today and the one developing in India—savings and capital spending become less crucial to sustaining growth. China saves and then invests an enormous percentage of its GDP in building new manufacturing capacity, which puts China at a real risk for over-capacity and deflation in the event of downturn (as we may be seeing already as this goes to press in early 2009). India, in contrast, appears to be skipping the industrial phase of its development altogether and moving directly to services and information, thus looking much more "American" than any other developing country.

India's demographics are slowly beginning to look more American as well. After decades of high birthrates and overpopulation, the country appears to be shifting away from the typical "Third World" population distribution in which perpetually high birthrates insure that the most productive members of society (primarily those aged 20 to 64) are a relatively small percentage of the population. The expense of raising this abundance of children (and the manpower taken out of the workforce to care for them) is an impediment to the development of a modern consumer economy, for better or worse.

Now, as more join the ranks of the middle class, Indian mothers are having fewer children, yet spending far more money on the ones they have, buying the basic consumer products that earlier generations simply had to do without. To see why this matters to the economy, think of it this way: profit margins are higher for store-bought disposable diapers than for home-made swaddling cloth. Add baby clothes, toys, and private piano lessons to the list of items purchased outside rather than produced at home, and it becomes obvious very quickly that a middle class lifestyle contributes far more to the economy than a traditional peasant one.

The leveling of the Indian birth rate is both an indication of the rise of the middle class as well as a contributing factor in its development. As India's birthrate continues to decline, the population distribution should start to look more and more like that of the US, circa 1964 (at the end of the American Baby Boom). Expect India to boom as its enormous young population begins to move through its Spending Wave over the next 40-50 years much like the American Baby Boomers of the post-war generation.

India's clout in the world economy will also continue to grow for another important reason. Unlike China, (whose total population is projected to peak around 2030) and Europe, Russia, and Japan (whose total populations have already peaked) India will continue to grow until approximately 2065.

Despite the overwhelmingly bullish case for India over the coming decades, it is important to remember that India is still an underdeveloped country and is at a much different stage than many other countries labeled as "developing," such as South Korea or Taiwan. Per capita income is still low, on par with Iraq or Cuba.

It is unlikely that India would ever follow the example of, say, Venezuela, and turn its back on the modern economic world, but there will definitely be setbacks that rattle investors. Even the United States, with its long tradition of free trade, has fallen into this trap recently, as the congressional revolt that killed the Dubai Ports deal in early 2006 and are threatening at time of writing to derail free-trade agreements with Peru, Panama, and Colombia make abundantly clear. Any political maneuvering in India or one of its major trading partners that undermines free trade could cause ugly, though most likely temporary, setbacks. India also has an unresolved conflict with Pakistan that could erupt into war at a moment's notice.

Still, all things considered, India looks to be the best candidate for the primary engine of global growth going forward. China is problematic for the reasons discussed in Chapter 4, and most of the other countries on the Eurasian landmass are too small individually to be significant world players. India is certainly the 800-pound gorilla of the group. Let us now take a look at some of the other significant emerging markets and offer our thoughts on their prospects.

The Country of the Future

Brazilians claim, tongue in cheek, that their country is the country of the future and that it always will be! Sadly, the same applies to virtually all of Latin America since its independence nearly 200 years ago. The region is rich in natural resources, and has a history of trade and commerce with the United States and Europe. Like the United States, parts of Latin America also have a long tradition of attracting immigrants and the new energy and innovation that immigrants often bring. Yet despite all of the human talent and natural potential, Latin America has largely been an economic disappointment.

To fully illustrate just how disappointing Latin America has been in recent decades, let us examine Figure 5.1. Mexico and Brazil were moving more or less in lockstep with the Asian tigers Taiwan and South Korea from the end of World War II until the early 1980s. Alas, it was not to continue. The two Latin heavyweight economies were utterly wrecked by the 1982 debt crisis that swept the region. Only recently has either country begun to gain traction again, a full two decades later. In fairness, Mexico did start to improve a little sooner, due in no small part to the boost in trade that the NAFTA agreement brought. But even with open access to the insatiable American consumer market next door, Mexico failed to achieve the growth rates needed to pull a poor country out of poverty.

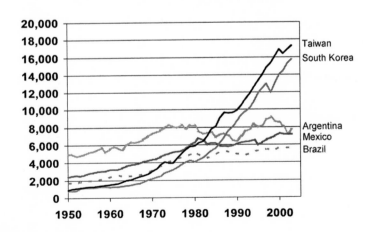

Real Per Capita GDP

Source: Angus Maddison

Figure 5.1: Real GDP Per Capita, Selected Countries

Meanwhile, Taiwan and South Korea have been able to maintain their stunning growth rates. Despite starting at even lower levels than Brazil or Mexico, these two countries have elevated their outputs to levels comparable to Europe. Though still classified as "emerging markets" in many indices, these countries now deserve a place at the table with Japan, Australia, and the other developed countries of the Pacific Rim. Both South Korea and Taiwan still rely too heavily on exports to the West—a relic of the state-guided "Asian development model" used first by Japan and still used by China. This is undesirable because it places these countries at the mercy of the West's economic health. As we discussed with respect to India, an economy that relies more on middle-class domestic consumption is a more stable economy. Still, as Figure 5.1 illustrates, South Korea and Taiwan have survived and prospered throughout the ups and downs of the global economy, and even the 1998 "meltdown" that struck the region failed to slow progress for long, nor did the dotcom bust in 2000. In due course, these regions will fall victim to the same demographic trends that will soon plague the West, and growth rates will slow markedly. Luckily, that day is still many years away.

Arguably the biggest failure of all emerging markets is Argentina, if only because the country had such a head start on the rest. Returning to Figure 5.1, we see that Argentina's per capita GDP was head and shoulders above the rest in 1950, about on par with Western Europe's. Fifty years later, Argentina's per capita GDP is barely a third of Western Europe's.

So what went wrong? Long after Hitler's and Mussolini's regimes were destroyed and their economic ideas discredited in Europe, they somehow found a new lease on life in Latin America. Juan Perón, the husband of Evita of Andrew Lloyd Webber fame, dominated Argentina's politics for most of the 1950s, 60s, and 70s, and still influences it from beyond the grave today. Argentina's government has oscillated between fascism and populism for most of the past 60 years. Not shockingly, the country's economic development has suffered as a result. This goes to show that, despite abundant human and natural resources and a history of trade and commerce, governmental policies can stunt growth. Just ask anyone who lived through the communist years in Russia or Eastern Europe.

Mao's communism in China and Nehru's socialism in India aside, Asia has been comparatively free of bad ideologies since the end of World War II. Though their state structures still seem somewhat intrusive by American standards, Japan, South Korea, Taiwan, and Singapore are firmly established as successful market-based economies. And with India and China now in the capitalist camp, political risk is less of a problem today. The region is still more problematic than, say, Europe or North America, but it appears to be heading in the direction of growth and stability.

Latin America is much more mixed. The ghost of Juan Perón appears to be firmly in control of Argentina. Even worse, Fidel Castro appears to be manipulating the puppet strings in Venezuela, Bolivia, Nicaragua, and in the opposition parties of numerous other countries. Castro and his ideology have somehow survived numerous assassination attempts and thousands of strong cigars to influence yet another generation.

Any attempt to do an economic analysis of Argentina, Venezuela, or Bolivia in 2008 would be an exercise in futility. There is simply too much political risk in our view. Plus, the dependence of the economy on commodity exports makes domestic consumption far less important. (The same is true in much of the Arab world and Africa).

That said, there are several bright spots in Latin America. Chile is a shining example of what is possible for the region. Mexico, Colombia, Brazil, and Peru are all also moving along the path of development, though all face unique, local problems. Regardless, all are building a significant middle class. As a further sign of progress, one of the chronic economic scourges that has wreaked havoc on the region for decades appears finally to be under control. The *Financial Times* recently reported that "Brazil has ended two years of interest rate cuts amid signs of returning inflationary pressure." So, is the country about to return to its days of 1,000% annual hyperinflation in a bout of populist social spending? Not a chance. The inflation rate that disturbed Brazil's central bank was a mere 3.9%, not far from the level recorded in the United States today.

Another piece of anecdotal evidence suggests that the region has reached a new economic plateau. The third and fourth quarters of 2008 were quite rough for the global economy. The subprime mortgage meltdown in the United States turned into a global liquidity crunch that sent ripples through the global economy and sent every major investment bank into crisis mode. Not long ago, such a crisis would have sent Brazil into a tailspin, but thus far the country appears to be weathering the storm nicely. International investors fled emerging markets in general, and this caused the Brazilian currency (the real) to fall slightly and its stock market to suffer a fairly significant correction. Still, the real remains near multi-year highs, and Brazilian stocks are still positive for the year. Government finances have never been healthier, and the central bank has a healthy stockpile of reserves. In Brazil (and Peru, Chile, and Colombia for that matter), the crisis that has American and European economists and money managers lying awake at night does not exist at all. It remains to be seen how these countries will fare during the next bear market in commodities, whenever it comes. Regardless, parts of the region have finally "come of age."

This is the factor that makes it possible to use Harry Dent's Spending Wave methodology. When a country reaches a level of urban/suburban, middle-class "mass affluence," demographic analysis begins to make sense. Mexico, Colombia, Brazil, and Peru are on the brink. All have populations that are over 70% urban, and all have established middle classes. Urban shoppers in these countries are more likely to go to the local equivalent of Wal-Mart to buy finished products than to a traditional peasant market to buy home-made goods. Unfortunately, all also have legions of poor who are outside of the economic mainstream. All things considered, we believe these countries are "close enough" to warrant a thorough Dent analysis.

In the sections to follow, we will consider the economic prospects of various countries around the world based on their demographic trends. We will focus our attention on emerging markets for reasons that will be obvious very quickly. We've already covered Japan in Chapter 3. To put it bluntly, Japan is dying. The population is aging rapidly and is already *shrinking*. We repeat: Japan's population is actually getting smaller. Japan's economy may get a mild rebound due to the economic reforms undertaken over the last decade and due to the country finally having worked off the excesses of its 1980s bubble. Also, Japan's echo boom, though relatively small, is beginning to reach its peak consumer spending years (refer to Figure 3.6 in Chapter 3). Still, Japan's overall economic prognosis is grim.

Western Europe Spending Wave

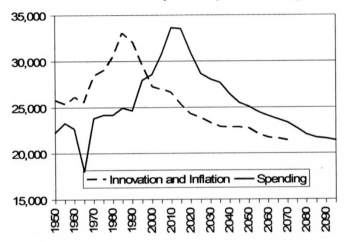

Source: HS Dent Foundation, from United Nations data

Figure 5.2: Western European Spending Wave

Likewise, as Figure 5.2 makes clear, Europe's best days of economic growth and stability will likely soon be behind her. Using the HS Dent Spending Wave methodology, we see that the number of Europeans entering their top spending years (aged 45-49) will reach a peak in 2010 and will then begin a long, perhaps terminal, decline. As far back as 1985, Europe passed her demographic peak for innovators (defined by HS Dent as 20-24-year olds).

To be sure, Europe still has potential. The continued economic integration of the European Union and the accompanying free-market reforms have the ability to unlock growth and efficiencies that have long been dormant. But, as Figure 5.2 should make obvious, the primary engine of the modern economy—consumer spending—may already be entering a decline that is likely to be permanent. Unless you intend to invest in sidewalk cafes or nursing homes, Europe is probably best avoided.

With that said, let us take a look at the prospect for major up-and-coming emerging economies.

A Look at Latin America

Of the Latin American countries with populations of significant size, Figures 3.3 through 3.7 outline the countries that we view as having the most potential: Brazil, Chile, Colombia, Mexico, and Peru. Each of these countries has made significant progress toward free-market economics and open democracy over the past decade. All appear to have largely abandoned the extreme radical populism that is currently plaguing Venezuela and Bolivia and have settled into civil, moderately left-wing administrations (Brazil, Chile, and Peru) or moderately right-wing administrations (Colombia and Mexico). Still, every country in the list is highly dependent on natural resources, and any protracted decline in the price of oil, copper, or other significant commodities could foreshadow an economic and political crisis. A regression into Venezuelan-style "Chavismo" cannot be ruled out. After all, within the past few years both Mexico and Peru have gone to the brink of electing radical authoritarian presidents before cooler heads eventually prevailed.

Brazil Spending Wave

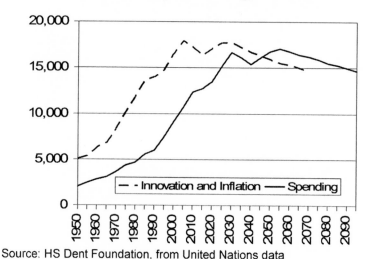

Source: HS Dent Foundation, from United Nations data

Figure 5.3: Brazil Spending Wave

Chile Spending Wave

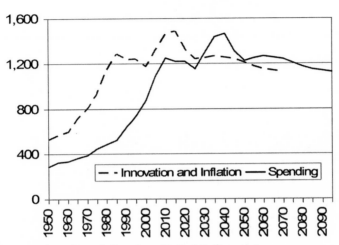

Source: HS Dent Foundation, from United Nations data

Figure 5.4: Chile Spending Wave

Colombia Spending Wave

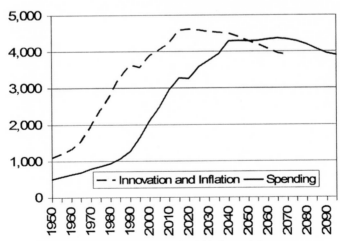

Source: HS Dent Foundation, from United Nations data

Figure 5.5: Colombia Spending Wave

Mexico Spending Wave

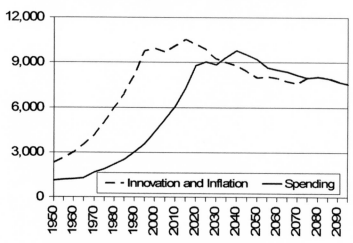

Source: HS Dent Foundation, from United Nations data

Figure 5.6: Mexico Spending Wave

Peru Spending Wave

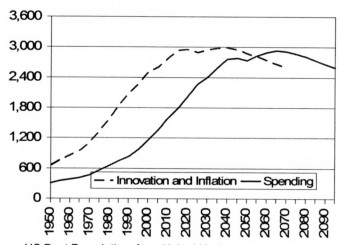

Source: HS Dent Foundation, from United Nations data

Figure 5.7: Peru Spending Wave

We believe that 2007 was the likely high-water mark for Latin socialism. Hugo Chavez's defeat in his constitutional referendum was a major turning point toward more moderate government and economics. But we cannot stress enough that political risk is still a major concern for the region and will be for a long time to come. Invest here, but do so carefully and with a full understanding of the risk.

Brazil, Colombia, and Peru have very similar demographic patterns. All are already highly urbanized and continue to see a large influx of economic migrants from the countryside to the cities. Most of these new migrants live in shanty towns and have incomes that would be considered below the poverty line virtually everywhere except Sub-Saharan Africa. Still, these migrants are firmly on the economic ladder, and evidence indicates that they are climbing, if slowly. Upon arriving in the cities, nearly all of these migrants abandon the trappings of their former agrarian peasant lifestyles and embrace the modern economy, including such superficial changes as replacing their traditional indigenous clothes with Western jeans and t-shirts. They also build and own their own homes, even if it is on untitled land[10]. They are dreaming what we would consider the middle-class "American" dream, even if they are starting at a lower economic level.

We shouldn't overly glorify these settlements, of course. These squatter ghettos are often full of crime and lack quality education and at times basic sanitation. Still, all three countries have demographic patterns that are favorable for consumer spending. As discussed above with India, city dwellers tend to have fewer children, yet spend much more money on the ones they do have. City dwellers buy finished manufactured goods; they buy their clothes in stores and markets rather than weaving them at home.

Brazil, Colombia, and Peru should all benefit from a continued boom in family consumer spending that is not likely to peak until well into the 2030s or even later. A lot can (and will) happen between now and then, and there will certainly be short-to-medium-term booms and busts. Still, the overall trend should be positive for decades to come.

Chile's demographic patterns are slightly different, but certainly

---

10   The Peruvian economist Hernando DeSoto has spent much of his career studying the effect on economic growth of securing legal title in squatter settlements, and we highly recommend his book *The Mystery of Capital.*

still very positive. As seen in Figure 3.4, the number of peak spenders will reach a medium-term plateau around 2010. This should take a couple points off of Chile's economic growth rate, but it will probably not be enough to send the country into the kind of demographic-based recession that Harry Dent has forecasted for the United States and Europe.

Chile is much further along the path of economic and political reform than the other major Latin economies due to the dominance of the "Chicago Boys" within General Pinochet's military government in the 1970s and 1980s. The country has also enjoyed a cash windfall during the 2000s due to the record-high world price of copper, Chile's principal export. Unless past regimes, which squandered the periodic windfalls from commodity booms, the current one has set aside the excess revenues into a stabilization fund for future needs that should shelter the country from the next inevitable bust in the price of copper. Furthermore, Chile will be largely immune from the pension/social security crisis that will soon overtake the United States and most of the rest of the world, as Chile's nationwide retirement system is structured like an American-style 401k or IRA, with individual accounts that are funded. While the rest of the world struggles to pay its past IOUs to retirees, Chile will be able to use its resources for future growth. Chile is, without a doubt, the shining star of Latin America.

Mexico is far more challenging. Despite its easy access to the enormous American market and cultural ties to the burgeoning Mexican American population, Mexico's growth and development have been disappointingly low. As the high levels of emigration to the United States make abundantly clear, Mexico's economy does not create enough quality jobs for its citizens.

Mexico has undertaken major reforms since the 1990s under presidents Zedillo, Fox, and Calderon. But unfortunately, the country still has a long way to go, and faces a problem that is all too common in Latin American. Reforming the economy in a "democratic" manner is nearly impossible, as far too many Mexican citizens have a stake in the status quo, and there will be major, organized resistance to any change. American presidents cannot think of reforming our own system of farm subsidies because they need the electoral votes of farming states like Iowa. If a small state like Iowa can effectively hold American agricultural policy hostage, imagine the political clout wielded by the millions of Mexican businesses and individuals that benefit from state patronage.

At the same time, "non-democratic" reform in the person of an authoritarian like Pinochet in Chile or Fujimori in Peru is not desirable either, for obvious reasons. The dictatorial power that would be necessary would open the door for a radical populist like Castro or Chavez to emerge and reverse any progress made.

Furthermore, Mexico's Spending Wave begins to plateau in 2020. If Mexico hopes to reform itself, it needs to happen in the next decade while demographic trends are still favorable.

Asia and Beyond

We have already covered the two giants of emerging Asia, China and India. The continent is full of other promising, demographically-young countries, but needless to say, China and India dominate. We'd now like to move our analysis to a region of the world that gets very little serious attention by investors and businesses, the greater Middle East.

There is no question that the energy sector dominates the economies of much of the region. For this reason, we will exclude Saudi Arabia, Iraq, Iran, Kuwait, and the Gulf sheikdoms from our analysis. After all, it really makes no difference what the demographic trends suggest for these countries, as ultimately *everything* revolves around oil revenues. In this chapter, we will limit our discussion to the two non-oil producing demographic heavyweights of the region, Turkey and Egypt.

Turkey has always been a country of contradictions. It straddles the divide between Europe and Asia, both geographically and culturally, yet does not fit cleanly into either. The Turks took the entire region by storm a millennium ago, riding in from the East and conquering Christian and Muslim alike, and it was only about ninety years ago that the Turks lost their Islamic empire. In the decades since the re-founding of the country as a secular republic, the primary motivation of the governing class has been the Westernization of the country. This was no easy task for a society of warlords who historically viewed both learning and commerce with disdain, but the project has been largely a success. Today Turkey has a GDP per capita about on par with Brazil, another emerging power and is home to one of the world's great cities, Istanbul. Turkey has also been a proud member of NATO since the early days of the Cold War, and has a customs union with the EU. Though still somewhat borderline, we believe Turkey is developed enough to warrant a Spending Wave analysis.

Turkey Spending Wave

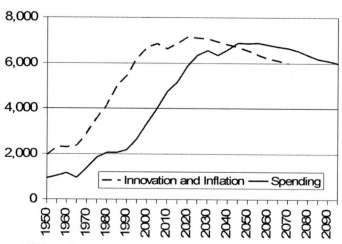

Source: HS Dent Foundation, from United Nations data

Figure 5.8: Turkey Spending Wave

Turkey's Spending Wave points to strong gains in consumer spending through 2030 with an ultimate peak around 2045. Should Turkey continue to develop economically and increase the purchasing power of its citizens, the country could be a major engine of demand for the entire European continent, including Russia. In a continent with aging demographics, Turkish workers and consumers could be a mitigating factor for Europe and could be an excellent destination for Western investment capital. For this to be viable though, several things must happen. Turkey must maintain its secular character and must maintain an open economy. The prognosis on this, unfortunately, is mixed.

The army is staunchly secular and pro-Western, and has been for almost a century. The army also wields considerable political power, both officially and "unofficially," as the generals have not been shy about threatening coups when they see the country drifting away from their ideal path. So, even while Turkey is currently ruled by a mildly Islamist political party (and likely will be for the next decade), the risk of the country drifting too far in the direction of political Islam is slim.

But oddly enough, it is the Islamist party that has adopted the best economic policies in recent decades. Under Prime Minister Recep Erdogan Turkey has pursued a policy of free markets and light (by Turkish standards) regulation. Much of Turkey's emerging class of entrepreneurs and small business owners is from the more religious hinterlands of the country, not the urbane city centers. These nouveau riche are an interesting blend of ideas: they are enthusiastic supporters of American-style capitalism but also conservative in their Islamic religious views. Meanwhile, the staunchly-secular army and the established political class have grown colder to the West, largely as a reaction to anti-Turkish sentiment in the EU and to fallout from the war in Iraq. Their economic views are also becoming increasingly nationalist and xenophobic, perhaps a milder version of similar trends in Russia and Venezuela.

This makes Turkey perhaps the biggest paradox in the world today: Somehow it is the Islamist party that is advocating Western-style democracy and capitalism while the secular and pro-Western army and political establishment are reverting to statism, autocracy, and a more closed economy.

We suspect that Turkey will weather this storm and will continue to grow and prosper. There will be hiccups along the way, of course. Within the past few years, the prime minister attempted to force a law through parliament that criminalized adultery, and the army came to the brink of toppling the government because the president-elect's wife wears a Muslim headscarf. Turks could also get frustrated by the lack of progress in obtaining EU membership, which is now looking increasingly unlikely, and do something self-defeating like halt the economic liberalization that has done so much for the country. Islamic fundamentalism could also be a nagging problem, as it has flared up at various points over the years.

Still, on balance Turkey looks like a good bet to us. There will be plenty of mini-crises, but we see Turkey having the best prospects in the greater Middle East region and in Eastern Europe as well.

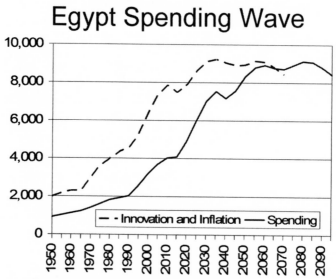

Source: HS Dent Foundation, from United Nations data

Figure 5.9: Egypt Spending Wave

The other demographic giant in the Middle East is, of course, Egypt. Unfortunately, we are much less enthusiastic about Egypt's economic prospects. To start, Egypt is starting from a much lower economic base. Egypt's GDP per capita is only $3,900, and its phone and internet penetration rates are barely a third of that of Turkey and about a sixth that of Spain. At this level of development, it is questionable whether a Spending Wave analysis is appropriate for Egypt. Egypt's Wave does point up strongly for the next fifty years, and this is a definite positive. Our fear is that the positive benefits of the Spending Wave will be overwhelmed by political instability, terrorism, and perhaps even anarchy and civil war when the current president dies. Furthermore, unlike some other authoritarian regimes like that of, say, China, the Egyptian government has shown no real desire to implement the reforms necessary to create a vibrant capitalist economy. Certainly, there has been progress made over the past decade, and this has been reflected in the strong performance of Egyptian stocks in recent years. But at this stage in the game, we view Egypt as being too unstable to consider for serious investment.

This concludes our "trip around the world." In the next chapter we will take a look at something near and dear to most American readers' hearts: the U.S. dollar. It's been a rough ride for the greenback thus far this decade. In chapter seven, we will offer our best insights as to what the future holds.

Chapter 6: The Future for the Dollar

The dollar is on the verge of collapse, which will make the cost of imports rise. China and Japan will soon begin dumping dollars on the currency markets, causing our interest rates to soar. The U.S. current account deficit will lead to Argentina-style hyperinflation. Millions will lose their savings and probably their homes as well. A third of the stars will fall out of the sky, and the Nile will turn to blood.

Ok, perhaps the last sentence was a bit of a stretch. But until very recently, the entire opening paragraph would have been considered absurd and would have been in the realm of tin-foil hats and conspiracy theory newsletters. Today, even blue-blooded financial newspapers are forecasting the doom of the dollar. Consider these recent headlines:

"Dollar Falls on Weak U.S. Data"

"Cashing in on the Weak Dollar "

"Dollar Falls Sharply on Tame Inflation"

"U.S. Dollar Slips on ISM Data"

It might be temping to blame the dollar's negative press coverage on the perceived leftward bias of the media or on the unpopularity of the Bush Administration, but all of the headlines above were posted in the *Wall Street Journal,* which is generally viewed as pro-Republican and supportive of the U.S. financial markets. And the *Journal* is not alone.

While respected dailies report on the dollar's decline, personal finance magazines and mainstream investment newsletters are busily advising their readership on ways to "diversify their dollar risk." The major banks and fund companies have certainly done their part as well, providing innovative new ETFs and mutual funds that allow investors to actively bet on the direction of the dollar. And for those investors who would rather not try their luck as currency speculators, it has never been easier to "get out" of the dollar indirectly by buying mutual funds and ETFs that track European, Asian, and emerging stock markets. Commodities (particularly gold and silver) have been aggressively marketed as "anti-dollars" as well.

Celebrated investors such as Warren Buffet have joined the party too. Mr. Buffet—the second richest man in the world and arguably the greatest investor in history—took a conspicuously large short position on the dollar in the early 2000s, which has paid off handsomely. Rank and file Americans have responded by plowing an unprecedented share of their investment dollars overseas and into alternative investments that promise to neutralize their risk to the U.S. markets and currency.

What are we to think of these developments? Is the dollar really doomed? Is this the beginning of a long-term secular trend in which Americans diversify a larger percentage of their portfolios abroad? Will American workers—like the Brazilian model Gisele Bundchen in November 2007—begin to demand their paychecks in euros?

The rumors of the dollar's death have been greatly exaggerated. It is our view that bearish sentiment on the dollar reached something close to hysteria in 2008. And as usually happens in moments of hysteria, at the moment of maximum pessimism a strange thing happened. While the credit markets collapsed and every major Wall Street investment bank either failed, merged, or converted to a commercial bank, the dollar actually rallied to a two-year high!

When *everyone* uniformly becomes bearish (or bullish), there is no one left to sell (or buy). The *Business Week* cover that announced the "Death of Equities" in 1979 proved to be such a laughingstock that we are still using it to mock the popular press nearly thirty years later. Jack Kennedy famously sold his equity holdings before the 1929 crash after receiving a stock tip from a shoe shine boy.

While the current extreme sentiment in the popular press and among average Americans regarding the dollar may not be quite on the level of these two examples, it is close. (After all, is taking currency advice from a Brazilian runway model any less absurd than taking stock tips from a New York shoeshine boy?) Despite the recent rally, sentiment towards the dollar remains almost universally negative.

A.B.U.S.E

It's not just dollars that are unloved these days. Writing for the *Financial Times*, Charles Biderman, founder and CEO of TrimTabs Investment Research, makes the tongue in cheek comment that investors are buying Abuse: "Anything But U.S. Equities." Mr. Biderman's view is supported by the facts. The *Journal* cites data from the Investment Company Institute that among Americans, *93% of net additions to stock funds in 2006 went to funds investing abroad!*

But the "abuse" does not stop here. Until the credit crisis hit, investors had been accompanying their new-found fascination with the stocks and bonds of countries they might normally have trouble finding on a map with commodities and alternative assets. The *Financial Times* reports that a full 13% of the world's silver output in 2006 was absorbed by a single ETF, the iShares Silver Trust. The buying pressure from this one fund alone was an enormous contributing factor to the 58% rise in the metal's price that year. Investor interest also contributed to the destruction of the roll yield in several commodities, most notably oil. Without going into the technical details, it has almost always been possible to earn a passive profit by rolling over oil futures contracts month-to-month. So, by following a passive "buy and hold" strategy with the futures contracts, investors could earn, say, 11-12% on their contracts while the actual oil price only rose, say, 10%. Over time, "total return" commodity indexes vastly outperform spot commodity prices. During the oil bubble, this was turned upside down. The shear volume of investor interest in commodity futures forced many (including oil) into contango, meaning that investors are actually *losing* money every month by rolling their contracts. Much of their profit from the recent spike in the oil price had been eroded, yet investors continued with this strategy, both institutional and individual investors alike. This is self "abuse" indeed!

We have actually saved the most extreme examples of "anything but stocks" for last. Fine wine has been one of the best performing "asset classes," up more than 100% in the past two years (Figure 6.1).

We use this term loosely, of course. A bottle of wine, no matter how satisfying, does not pay dividends or interest, nor does it have any industrial use. Yet demand has been strong enough to warrant the creation of an investment fund, the Vintage Wine Fund. According to Dr. Steve Sjuggerud, the fund has over $67 million in assets.

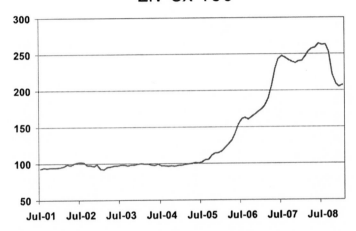

Source: www.liv-ex.com

Figure 6.1: Fine Wine Index

Perhaps the most bizarre investment idea to date is the Fine Violins Fund. Yes, there is now a hedge fund that does nothing but trade collectable violins. According to the *Financial Times*, the fund has a target return of 8-12% and also has a secondary philanthropic objective: "The historic violins it buys will be lent to up-and-coming musicians, contributing to the instruments' value and helping prevent woodworm." Wine and violin connoisseurs were no doubt annoyed as their collectables were bid to unreasonable prices and locked in the vaults of banks.

The rise in "exotic" asset classes and the disdain for U.S. assets in general was an understandable reaction to the bear market of 2000-2002 and to the lack of value in the bond market. Investors were loath to get back into the same stocks that had burned them before, and as we discuss later in the book, bonds offered little in the way of yield.

This lead investors to emerging markets and commodities and also to hedge funds Paying "2 and 20" for an exotic hedge fund suddenly seemed reasonable given the lack of quality options out there.

Much the same is true of the dollar. Due perhaps to disgust with their losses, investors looked to get out of the dollar altogether. Certainly, after roughly a decade of a "strong dollar," it was natural that the greenback revert to the mean. As often happens during mean reversions, the dollar overshot in its decline and became very weak for several years.

Developed-market currencies like the dollar, yen, pound sterling, and the euro (or the old German deutschmark) tend to follow relatively long bull and bear cycles. After nearly a decade of erosion, the dollar was due for a new bull market. It's too early to say if the current dollar rally we are in is the start of a new long-term bull market or if it is purely a result of the deleveraging process plaguing the global financial system.

Portfolio Strategies

We will establish in later chapters the need for international diversification in stock and bond portfolios. Many advisors will point out that this creates currency risk. But isn't that the point? Doesn't currency risk also imply the potential for returns? Yes, absolutely. Over time, currency fluctuations tend to cancel each other out, so your dollar losses are compensated by, say, euro gains, or vice versa. Plus, for all the talk of the new "flat world" of globalization, international markets are not perfectly integrated and probably never will be. (Heston and Rouwenhorst's 1994 paper analyzes this phenomena in detail) *In other words, factors that are specific to individual countries still matter.* These include powerful long-term trends like demographics and shorter-term factors like government and central bank policies and acts of terrorism.

Regular, disciplined portfolio rebalancing can allow you to profit from these fluctuations by continually buying low and selling high within the context of your strategic allocation. Tactical speculations can add value as well, though it is important to have a strategic allocation as your foundation.

Part II: Mitigating a Potential Retirement Disaster

Strategies for State, City, and Local Governments Struggling to Meet the Retirement and Health Needs of the Largest Generation in U.S. History

Chapter 7: The Healthcare Time Bomb

When the Governmental Accounting Standards Board ("GASB") announced the GASB 45 guidelines in 2004, U.S. state and local government officials cringed. Anyone familiar with government finances knew that there would be some unintended consequences. For years, state and local governments had been able to quietly ignore the accumulating healthcare liabilities promised to their workers (technically called "OPEB," or Other Post Employment Benefits). The amount due in the current year was dutifully paid, but the value of the total accumulated debt to eventually be paid was rarely if ever mentioned beyond the footnotes of the financial statements. It certainly didn't show up on the balance sheet as an outstanding debt. The governments, their taxpayers, and even the bond rating agencies seemed content to leave this issue unresolved.

Despite the implementation of GASB 45, some governments have continued to insist that ignorance is bliss. In May, the Texas legislature actually voted to "opt out" of complying with the accounting standard. The second-largest state in the Union voted to thumb its nose at a recognized government accounting convention, believing that a state as big as Texas was too big for the ratings agencies to downgrade. The state Comptroller, representing Texas's position to GASB, defended the move by claiming that the state's health benefits were not true obligations, per se, because they were not contractual and can be changed at the will of the legislature. Of course, the legislature has not "willed' to reduce these benefits because doing so would be extremely unpopular with current and retired state workers, who happen to make up a large voting block.

The *Wall Street Journal* offered a great analogy. Officials are "pretending the animal does not exist—even while they continue to feed it under the table."

So, exactly how big *is* this OPEB issue?

The Great GASB

First, some background is appropriate. GASB 45, *Accounting and Financial Reporting by Employers for Postretirement Benefits Other than Pensions*, was designed to make public-sector accounting better reflect reality and accurately disclose long-term obligations. With the glaring exception of the Social Security system, public-sector pensions have historically been managed and accounted for in much the same way as company pensions. A dedicated fund of assets is set aside to be managed of behalf of the pension beneficiaries. Unfunded shortfalls appear on the balance sheet of the sponsor as a liability, representing debts that must be paid.

OPEB accounting has always been a little hazier. Rather than set aside a dedicated pool of assets to meet these liabilities, state and local governments (as well as most companies) chose to expense these costs on a pay-as-you-go basis, making them the accounting equivalent of salaries or office supplies. The problem is, OPEB is nothing at all like current salaries and supplies. Employees are paid for current work. When employees resign, those expenses disappear in the next period. Retiree healthcare obligations, however, don't disappear. They grow. And unlike pension plans, in which plan assets are expected to grow more or less as fast as liabilities, these obligations are generally unfunded. Not just *under*funded like many state pensions, but *un*funded. **Generally, there are no assets set aside at all.**

To explain why the state of Texas was reluctant to disclose to its creditors and taxpayers the full extent of its OPEB liabilities, the *Wall Street Journal* estimates that the state's healthcare obligations are over $50 billion, including city and county governments[11]. **Nationwide, the estimates for the unfunded liabilities range from $1.5 trillion to $2 trillion**[12].

State by State, Blow by Blow

Texas has thus far proven to be the most openly defiant, but the Lone Star State's finances are far from being the worst in the Union. Texas is roughly in the middle of the pack.

---

11   "Accounting, Texas-Style" *Wall Street Journal*, May 29, 2007

12   Ibid and "You Dropped a Bomb on Me, GASB." Special Report by Credit Suisse, March 22, 2007

To get an idea of the kinds of numbers we're talking about, let's take a bird's eye view. In a recent report, Credit Suisse made estimates of unfunded health liabilities for state governments. The largest are outlined in Figure 7.1. California, Texas, Washington, and most of the Eastern states have unfunded health liabilities in excess of $10 billion. California tops the charts at an estimated $70 billion, which is understandable given that California has both the largest population and the largest economy of all the states. It's also not surprising to find Texas and New York in the top four for the same reasons. Yet somehow, tiny New Jersey has managed to make the number two spot, and North Carolina finds itself at five! It is equally disturbing to find small states like Connecticut on the list. How can a state that is scarcely bigger than the Atlanta metro area owe more in retiree health expenses than the entire state of Georgia?

Est. OPEB Underfunding by State (2007)

State	Estimated OPEB Underfunding
California	$70,000
New Jersey	$60,000
New York	$54,000
Texas	$26,817
North Carolina	$23,786
Maryland	$22,903
Michigan	$22,745
Connecticut	$21,100
Alabama	$20,000
Georgia	$20,000
	US$ in millions

Source: Credit Suisse 2007

Figure 7.1: Estimated OPEB Underfunding by State

For a fair comparison, let's look at the OPEB liabilities on a per capita basis. Figure 7.2 lists the states with the biggest potential crises. New Jersey, Connecticut, Alabama, and Maryland are familiar names from Figure 7.1. But any of the states on this list face significant challenges ahead. Using New Jersey as an example, an OPEB liability of

$6,877 *per person* means that every family of four "owes" $27,508 just to fund the retirement health benefits of state workers, not including the health benefits of city, county, and federal workers.

Largest OPEB Underfunding per Capita (2007)

State	Estimated OPEB Underfunding	Population	OPEB Underfunding per Capita
Alaska	$4,722	670053	$7,047
New Jersey	$60,000	8724560	$6,877
Connecticut	$21,100	3504809	$6,020
Hawaii	$5,654	1285498	$4,398
Alabama	$20,000	459030	$4,349
West Virginia	$7,781	1818470	$4,279
Maryland	$22,903	5615727	$4,078
Delaware	$3,175	853476	$3,720
Maine	$4,756	1321574	$3,599
Kentucky	$13,425	4206074	$3,192
	US$ in millions		US$ in millions

Source: Credit Suisse (2007)

Figure 7.2: Estimated OPEB Underfunding by State Per Capita

If you currently receive health benefits from one of these states, be prepared for the very real possibility that your benefits may be cut or reduced. If you live in one of these states, be prepared to pay higher sales and/or property taxes. If you are in the unenviable position of state treasurer, get ready for some lean years. You will face severe budgetary constraints in the coming years as your liabilities grow much faster than your tax base. The kinds of large-scale tax revolts associated with California can probably be expected as well, given the size of the obligations per person. Be ready.

Given that many Americans struggle to pay for their own health insurance in this age of soaring premiums and deductibles, it is a little unrealistic to expect them to tolerate a tax hike in order to fund the retirement health expenses of *others*. At the same time, those benefits were promised to the state workers and retirees as part of their employment, so they are within their legal rights to feel entitled to them. Remember, most states are operating on tight budgets, and taxpayers are already burdened with high property and sales taxes, among others. And unlike the federal government, the states do not have the ability to print money in the event of a financial pinch. There will be an inevitable bitter political fight between taxpayers, labor unions and retirees in the coming years, and none are likely to walk away happy.

Of course, there is a "third way" that wouldn't involve unpopular tax hikes or benefit cuts. The states could simply issue long-term bonds and use the cash proceeds to create something resembling a pension fund. The assets, if invested well, could grow at a faster rate than the liabilities, giving the states flexibility. Another option might be for the states to sell toll roads, bridges, and other infrastructure assets to private investors for cash upfront. This process has been perfected by the Australian Macquarie Bank, which has created a number of public and private infrastructure investment funds. Unfortunately, none of these options is ideal.

We'll start with the bond option. The main problem with this is that the dollar amount is simply too high to be feasible. Consider the case of Alabama in Figure 7.3. The state currently has $1.2 billion in debt…but $20 billion in estimated OPEB liabilities! *This means that Alabama would have to multiply its existing state debt by a factor of 16 times in order to fund its OPEB liabilities!*

Estimated OPEB Underfunding (2007)

State	Estimated OPEB Underfunding	Long-Term Debt	%
Alabama	$20,000	$1,270	1574%
Maine	4,756	1,063	447%
Idaho	2,314	564	410%
North Carolina	23,786	6,519	365%
Michigan	22,745	6,300	361%
Kentucky	13,425	4,100	327%
Delaware	3,175	1,027	309%
South Dakota	1,320	427	309%
Vermont	1,419	461	308%

Source: Credit Suisse (2007)

Figure 7.3: OPEB Underfunding vs. Debt

Clearly, Alabama is not the norm. But as Credit Suisse reports, 31 of the 50 states have OPEB liabilities that are larger than their official state debts. This means that the average state's recorded debt will at least double with OPEB recognition. We repeat: *the average state's official debt will more than double when retiree health benefits are recognized.*

What might this do to the credit ratings of these states? Might a downgrade or two be reasonable? Many Americans personally fund their retirements with tax-free state municipal bonds. Just ask holders of Ford and GM bonds what happens when the bond issuer suffers a downgrade. It's not pretty! So, we can add the proverbial "widows and orphans" who depend on bonds to fund their living expenses to the list of people likely to be hurt when the value of their municipal bonds suffer due to ratings downgrades.

As for sales of assets such as toll roads or bridges (which is not a legal options for many state and local governments), how many toll roads would you have to sell to cover a *$20 billion* deficit? Furthermore, these kinds of assets, if properly managed, can provide stable income for the governments that own them. They are less volatile than sales and income taxes, which can be quite erratic depending of the phase of the economy. Does it make sense to sell assets like these? Perhaps. There is much to be said about the economic benefits to privatization, though there have been a few blunders as well. The states that privatize their infrastructure assets may regret doing so when they run out of assets to sell.

There is also a second problem with attempting to pre-fund these health liabilities with either debt or asset sales. In their annual report on state retirement systems, Wilshire and Associates reveals the current asset allocation of state pensions[13] (Figure 7.4). (We assume that state healthcare funds, if set up, would follow a comparable allocation.)

---

13   2007 Wilshire Report on State Retirement Systems: Funding Levels and Asset Allocation

Average Asset Allocation for State Pension Plans

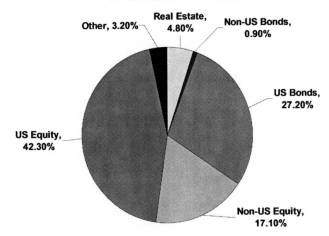

Source: Wilshire Report on State Retirement Systems

Figure 7.4: Asset Allocation of State Pension Plans

Equities make up nearly 60% of the state pension assets. This makes sense for long-term liabilities given that stocks have returned 7-10% per year (depending on the source), easily outperforming bonds and other assets.

The problem is, we just had a spectacular bear market in United States that may persist for several years, based on the forecasts of the HS Dent Foundation. States have contributed massive sums of cash to the stock market…just as it enters a decade-long bear market. This would be a repeat of the pension funding crisis that plagued most pensions after the 2000-2002 bear market, only this time the funds are unlikely to be "bailed out" by a subsequent bull market like the one enjoyed from 2003 to 2007. This is not likely to end well.

It's Not Just the States That Face a Problem

We've spent most of this discussion analyzing the states, but the states are only the beginning. A quick look at the obligations faced by local governments reveals more of the same. As Figure 7.5 reveals,

New York City owes a staggering *$50 billion* in healthcare liabilities to retirees. Given the strength of the public sector unions in New York, the city will not have an easy time negotiating these down. Even a small city like El Paso, Texas has managed to promise over *half a billion dollars* in OPEB to its city retirees. Depending on the existence and strength of unions in each city, some cities will have an easier time negotiating benefit cuts than others. At any rate, local governments face enormous challenges in the years ahead. Get ready.

Estimated OPEB Underfunding for the 25 Largest Cities (in millions)

City	State	Estimated OPEB Underfunding	City	State	Estimated OPEB Underfunding
New York City	NY	$50,544	Phoenix	AZ	$1,359
Detroit	MI	$6,477	Austin	TX	$1,203
San Francisco	CA	$4,948	Denver	CO	$1,194
Philadelphia	PA	$2,952	Seattle	WA	$1,061
Baltimore	MD	$2,727	Columbus	OH	$814
Memphis	TN	$2,669	Miwaukee	WI	$792
Houston	TX	$2,207	Charlotte	NC	$577
Boston	MA	$2,088	El Paso	TX	$573
Los Angeles	CA	$1,758	Fort Worth	TX	$564
San Antonio	TX	$1,626	San Jose	CA	$372
Dallas	TX	$1,492	Indianapolis	IN	$46
Chicago	IL	$1,400	Jacksonville	FL	$0
San Diego	CA	$1,380			

Source: Credit Suisse

Figure 7.5: Estimated OPEB Underfunding for the 25 Largest Cities

Of course, the sums promised by the federal government in the form of Medicare dwarf all other layers of government. We are not talking about federal employees; we are talking about the entire country!

Figure 7.6 outlines the financial position of the federal government. During the 2008 election season, the $10.4 trillion in government debt was thrown around as a scare statistic by both parties, as it rightfully should be. $10 trillion is a lot of money. But compared to the Medicare liabilities, the $10 trillion in debt is loose change. *Combined Medicare obligations total to more than $32 trillion!*

Major Fiscal Exposures

($ trillions)

	2006
Explicit liabilities	**$10.4**
–Publicly held debt –Military & civilian pensions & retiree health –Other	
Commitments & contingencies	**1.3**
–E.g., PBGC, undelivered orders	
Implicit exposures	**38.8**
–Future Social Security benefits	6.4
–Future Medicare Part A benefits	11.3
–Future Medicare Part B benefits	13.1
–Future Medicare Part D benefits	7.9
Total	**$50.5**

Source: 2006 Financial Report of the US Government

Figure 7.6: Major Fiscal Exposures

It is important not to fall into the trap of extrapolation. Clearly, these are impossible numbers. Medicare liabilities alone are estimated at more than ten times our current federal budget, and this says nothing about Social Security or other large programs. At some point, it all begins to sound like Monopoly money. Cuts will be made because full payment will be impossible.

This sounds good, of course, until you realize that a cutback to the Medicare obligation is money taken out of *your* Medicare entitlement once your reach retirement age. This means that you, and every other American, will be paying more out of pocket for your health and insurance needs in retirement. You will also likely be paying more in taxes as well.

More money spent on healthcare and taxes means less money to be spent on golf or flights to visit the grandkids. The money has to come from somewhere; it won't, as Fed Chairman Ben Bernanke once joked, fall out of a helicopter into our yards. And even if money *did* fall out of a helicopter into our yards, the result would be inflation and rising prices with no increase in purchasing power…so we'd be back to square one.

In an attempt to give us all a "free lunch," our various levels of government have assured that at least some of us will be left with a very expensive dinner bill.

Chapter 8: Moral Hazard at the Doctor's Office

No, this section has nothing to do with stem cell research or doctor-assisted suicide. Moral hazard is a very real phenomenon whenever people are shielded from the consequences of their decisions. It is a particular problem in the case of insurance. Consider the recent and high-profile case of the Hurricane Katrina disaster in New Orleans. Is it wise for builders or city planners to allow homes to be built below sea level and next to a levee? Of course not. But as long as the insurance company or the government pays the bill in the event of disaster, who cares? Despite every warning not to, much of the flood-prone areas of New Orleans are busily being rebuilt.

Banking is another fine example. Before the Great Depression, there were few protections on your savings other than the good reputation of the bank holding them. A prudent saver in that era would only deposit his or her hard-earned cash in a conservative, safe institution. Unfortunately, the Depression nearly took down the entire banking system, good and bad banks alike. As a result, we now have FDIC federal insurance that protects your savings in the event of bank failure. Most economists view the development of FDIC insurance as a good thing, in that it encourages savers to take their cash out from under the mattress and put it into the financial system, where it can be used to fund economic growth. Of course, the very same economists would add the caveat that this insurance also has the effect of encouraging excessive risk taking and general carelessness by depositors. After all, why bother investigating the bank's solvency if the government is the one shouldering the risk?

"But," you might protest, "there are costs to the consumer. Homeowners pay more for insurance premiums after major claims are filed and we all pay more in taxes after a federal 'bail out' of a failed bank."

Yes, this is true. ***But the incremental cost to each individual is***

small relative to the cost to the system as a whole. Sure, you may pay a couple hundred extra dollars per year in flood insurance premiums. But the insurance company had to shell out many *thousands* of dollars to repair or rebuild your house. This is moral hazard in action.

Believe it or not, the situation is even worse when it comes to healthcare, for a number of reasons. First, healthcare, rightly or wrongly, has a sense of entitlement that other expenses simply do not have. People believe that they have a right to healthcare, or at the very least, a right "not to die." The idea that cost is irrelevant when it comes to saving or improving lives leads to higher costs. Adding to this is the fact that Medicare is the ultimate payer in many cases, and most people (again, rightly or wrongly) seem to have no moral qualms with leaving a large medical bill for the government to pay. Most patients probably do not even realize that they are doing it.

For perhaps the best analogy to the moral hazard issue, consider Richard Epstein's analogy of teenagers sharing a soda:

> Think of two ways in which a group of 10 teenagers can drink soda at a luncheon counter. One is to get a large pitcher and have 10 thirsty kids each use a straw to take out what he or she wants. The second is to divide the soda into glasses, and assign them one to a person. Let there be 10 pints and each teenager's initial entitlement is one pint either way. The patterns of consumption of the soda will not be the same in these two arrangements. Even if by some miracle each person gets the same amount of soda in the two configurations (which they won't), we can be 100 percent confident that the soda will be more rapidly consumed when all 10 teenagers slurp their soft drink from the common pitcher. Consumption rates will slow markedly if each has his or her own glass, for slow sipping now results in greater satisfaction, not a reduction in individual share.
>
> **—Richard A. Epstein**
> Foreword to *Medicare Meets Mephistopheles*[14]

---

14   Hyman, David A. *Medicare Meets Mephistopheles*. New York, NY: The Cato Institute, 2006.

During the 1990s, there was an enormous public backlash against "Hillarycare," because Americans were not ready at the time for socialized medicine. The truth, however, is that we largely *already have* socialized medicine in the form of Medicare, and not just for those over the age of 65. In a recent editorial, *The Wall Street Journal* went so far as to call it "Soviet" medicine. While it may be bit of an exaggeration to compare Medicare to the situation in the old USSR, the *Journal* notes some similarities:

> The essential problem is this. The pricing of medical care in this country is either directly or indirectly dictated by Medicare; and Medicare uses an administrative formula which calculates 'appropriate' prices based upon imperfect estimates and fudge factors. Rather than independently calculate prices, private insurers in this country almost universally use Medicare prices as a framework to negotiate payments. [15]

Market prices set by a governmental planning authority? Come to think of it, that *does* sound rather Soviet.

This adds an entirely new element to the moral hazard that plagues the industry. Not only do patients push all responsibility for controlling costs into the hands of insurance companies, but the companies themselves push all of the responsibility into the hands of Medicare! If an insurance company is overcharged for a routine procedure, they can simply raise premiums on the patient's insurance plan and then blame the Medicare pricing scheme for the whole debacle. In the case of company-sponsored plans, an additional level of unaccountability is added, given that the premiums are paid by the company, not the user of the insurance. Because none of the players involved has any incentive to exercise discipline, it's no shock that *"excessive and unjustified costs consume as much as 20% of health care spending."*[16] With no real responsibility at any point in the chain, what *is* shocking is that our system isn't even more dysfunctional that it is.

---

15   Swerlick, Robert A. "Our Soviet Health System." *Wall Street Journal*, June 5, 2007.

16   "Slicko." *Forbes*, August 13, 2007.

The Mechanics of Moral Hazard

In review, moral hazard is the problem that arises when one person gets the benefits and someone else pays the bill. One of the best explanations of the phenomenon to date was Mark Pauly's 1968 paper published in the *American Economic Review*.[17] One of the points that Mr. Pauly emphasizes (and that we reiterate in this report) is that health insurance offers incentives for patients to over-consume healthcare. True insurance is designed to protect the policyholder from random, unpredictable, and catastrophic events, such as your house being struck by lightning; insurance is not designed to pay for routine house painting and maintenance. Yet somehow, these same principals have been lost in health insurance. We don't buy health insurance just to protect ourselves from catastrophic diseases, such as cancer. We also use it for yearly flu shots and amoxicillin, the medical equivalents of painting and routine maintenance. In practice, it appears that we do not view health insurance as insurance at all, but rather as a medical pre-paid card. More accurately, it could be described as a gift certificate, in that we end up buying things that we never would buy normally if we were using our *own* money. The result is that we over-consume on expenditures that are often frivolous and drive the price higher than it needs to be.

Pauly writes:

> [In order for health insurance to be optimal], the costs of medical care must be random variables. But if such expenses are not completely random, the proposition no longer holds. **The quantity of medical care an individual will demand depends on his income and tastes, how ill he is, and the price charged for it** *(emphasis ours).* The effect of an insurance which indemnifies against all medical care expenses is to reduce the price charged to the individual at the point of service from the market price to zero.

Whether insurance encourages over-consumption depends on the elasticity of demand for healthcare. To translate "economist speak," the elasticity of demand refers to how flexible your purchase decision is. Your demand for food is inflexible; you need it to live. But your

---

17   Pauly, Mark V. "The Economics of Moral Hazard." *The American Economic Review*, Vol. 58, No. 3, Part 1 (June 1968), pp. 531-537.

demand for, say, beef is very flexible. If it gets too expensive, you can buy chicken instead.

Demand for Healthcare

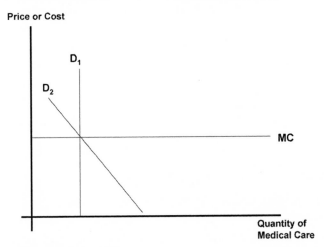

Source: Adapted from Pauly 1968

Figure 8.1: Demand for Healthcare

Figure 8.1 illustrates this situation graphically. Line D_1 is an example of inelastic demand. As you can see, the amount of healthcare demanded is the same at all price levels. This is pretty close to reality for life-saving procedures, such as an emergency heart bypass surgery. Most medical decisions look a lot more like D_2, however. On line D_2, the amount of care demanded decreases as the price increases. There are quite a few noncritical medical procedures you might be willing to forgo were the price high enough. They might be highly desirable, but at some price they are just not financially worth it. This is where over-consumption and moral hazard comes into play. As Pauly continues:

> Each individual may well recognize that 'excess' use of medical care makes the premium he must pay rise. No individual will be motivated to restrain his own use, however, since the incremental benefit to him for excess use is great, while the additional cost of his use is largely spread over other insurance holders, and so he bears only a tiny fraction of the cost of his use.

This is Epstein's pitcher-of-soda analogy in action. The teenagers end up drinking more soda and drinking it faster with little if any effect on their portion of the lunch tab. So what's the solution? Abolish all forms of insurance? Doing so would eliminate moral hazard and almost definitely lower prices, but is that really what we want? Most people lack the financial means to pay for major surgeries and life-saving treatments when they became necessary. Clearly, some kind of insurance is needed. Pauly suggests restricting insurance to cover only catastrophic and relatively random illnesses. This is consistent with new products such as Health Savings Accounts ("HSAs"), which combine a high-deductible insurance policy with a tax-advantaged savings account. Because the *patient's* money and not the insurance company's money is at stake, patients and doctors alike are likely to use a little more discipline. The result should be twofold: value conscious consumers who are more engaged and ultimately lower medical bills, lower premiums, and fewer overworked doctors.

While any form of insurance is bound to introduce moral hazard into the system, this is not entirely bad. As Clark Havighurst explains, "A degree of moral hazard is a natural concomitant of any arrangement, private or public, that gives people security about their future health care costs. Because such financial security is valuable to people, it is not irrational to incur some higher costs to obtain it."[18] Well said, and we agree completely. The key will be to keep the costs of moral hazard in the health industry to a tolerable minimum, especially given the demands that our system will face as the Boomers age and require ever-increasing amounts of care. For any system to be viable with a looming burden as large as the one we face, there must be a mechanism to make consumers more financially accountable for the services they use. Unfortunately, this means that higher out-of-pocket healthcare costs for consumers are virtually guaranteed.

---

18   Havighurst, Clark C. *Health Care Choices.* Washington, DC: The AEI Press, 1995.

Chapter 9: OPEB Mitigation Strategies

Chapter concepts and strategy provided by Genesis America's VEBA

"The definition of insanity is doing the same thing over and over and expecting different results"
-- Benjamin Franklin

Like a tiny ripple that swells into a devastating tsunami, retiree healthcare costs may overwhelm most government agencies in just a few short years. The rising tide of soon-to-be retired Baby Boomers expecting their promised benefits will be tapping into an already tight pool of government funds.

This issue is a complex one that ties in several themes discussed in prior chapters. First, the impending retirement of the Baby Boomers should be a concern for us all but it is particularly worrisome for governmental agencies because the average age of a government worker tends to be much older than the workforce as a whole. Figure 9.1 gives an example. Consider the difference in the age distribution of San Francisco compared to the United States as a whole. Many old-line "Rust Belt" industries, such as automakers, are facing a similar situation. Younger workers have migrated to newer, more dynamic industries such as technology and finance, while their parents or older siblings remain in the "old economy" and in government. In other words, Silicon Valley and Wall Street are not facing a retiree problem any time soon, but the governments of San Francisco and New York City certainly are!

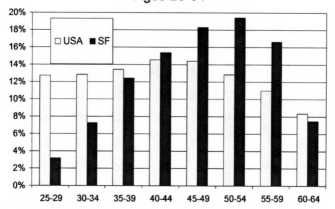

Age of Workforce
San Francisco Public Workers vs.
US Population Average
Ages 25-64

USA ■ SF

25-29 30-34 35-39 40-44 45-49 50-54 55-59 60-64

Source: San Francisco Controller's Office, United Nations

Figure 9.1: San Francisco Employee Age vs. U.S. Average

Another problem is that of "moral hazard," as discussed in Chapter 8. Healthcare costs are out of control for several reasons, including lack of accountability at all levels: from the patient, to the providers, to the insurance company, and even to Uncle Sam (and ultimately to us all as taxpayers and voters). Benefit promises have been made to government workers by politicians and bargaining units with, shall we say, "short time horizons." A congressman or city councilman can vote today to increase benefits in the interest of avoiding labor unrest or winning votes, but that politician will likely be retired from politics by the time those promises come due. This is a variation of moral hazard: a politician can vote to "rob Peter to pay Paul" and there is virtually no personal cost to the politician. But there are consequences for future generations because there is a time component. A more apt metaphor would be that the politician is robbing Peter's yet-to-be-born grandchildren by promising Paul's generous retirement today. This is a fundamental problem of government defined-benefit health plans. Future generations are committed to paying for past and present obligations.

When you combine already soaring costs, an enormous demographic tidal wave, and promises to pay for it all regardless of cost, you are looking at a perfect storm.

The open-ended legacy promise to pay for retiree medical care is riding heavily on the backs of employers and local governments. It is the concept of a *defined* benefit promise that is the real rub here. Many governments have offered their workers (and even their spouses and dependents!) 100% insurance coverage *for life* in retirement. Unless something is done, government agencies will find themselves solely in the business of providing employee benefits, with little money available to provide community services, maintain roads, and fund police and fire departments.

We're having a GASB!

The accounting standard GASB 45 (discussed in Chapter 7) can be compared to a family planning for a baby. You have a child today and want the child to attend college 18 years later. Unless the baby is born with a trust fund from a rich relative, this is an unfunded liability. Simplifying the math, you figure out how much 4 to 6 years of college is going to cost and divide by the 18 years until that child starts school. Then, discounting that stream of annual savings by the assumed investment return gives you the Annual Required Contribution (ARC). In other words, the total of the annual contributions plus investment return adds up to the value of that future liability—sending junior off to college. (For those of you that are unfamiliar with the finance terms, think of it this way: if you pawn your watch today, the pawn shop owner will give you a discounted price today, but when you return a month later to buy your watch back, you pay back the full price).

How can the obligation be reduced?

As established in Chapter 7, the health benefits owed by governments are astronomical. But, these liabilities can be reduced. A GASB 45 OPEB mitigation strategy can include a variety of risk management and funding techniques:

1. Reduce cost of current benefit offerings by: modifying eligibility, capping contributions, and/or limiting future promises and/or asking employees to pay a higher percentage of the monthly premium.

2. Transition from employees a *defined benefit* to *defined contribution* approach. (Regulatory standards apply to employers sponsoring OPEB plans through a defined benefit approach **but *not*** to those sponsoring OPEB plans through a defined contribution approach.)

3. Sunset defined benefit promises.

4. Implement a consumer-directed health plan.

5. Pre-fund defined benefit OPEBs to enable the use of a long-term discount rate during actuarial valuation.

6. Explore alternative funding sources.

We will explore each of these strategies in the sections below.

GASB Mitigation, Step by Step

First, and most obviously, it is essential to reduce the cost of the benefit in some meaningful way. One popular way to do this is to modify employee eligibility by extending the length of employee service required for vesting. Instead of offering immediate vesting from the first day of employment, require employees to work 5, 10 or even 20 years before they are eligible. Another option, cap or limit the amount of benefits to a specific dollar amount, with or without an adjustment for inflation. Obviously, it's better for the employer if there is no inflation adjustment.

Second, follow the lead of most corporate and government pension providers by moving from a defined benefit approach to a *defined contribution.* While there are specific IRS funding requirements, the concept behind a defined contribution is fairly simple. An employer simply contributes dollars into an employee's individual investment account, often called a Retiree Medical Savings Accounts ("RMSA"). With this solution the employee can later access this money for medical expenses during his or her post retirement years. Think of RMSA—see box—as employer contribution 401k plans that are structured to reimburse eligible medical expenses and premiums during retirement. The biggest advantage, for the employee, funds deposited, interest earned and the distributions from the account are often *tax-free.*

One of the fundamental problems with the current healthcare arrangement is that the retiree's former employer shoulders an open-ended liability that lasts as long as the retiree (and possibly spouse) lives. It's like a parent having an adult child that they have to support indefinitely. In a defined contribution approach, you effectively give the child a small trust fund and then cut him off. (We'll discuss this in more detail in Step 4, Consumer-Directed Plans.) This is the key to reducing future open-end legacy costs while still offering a viable way for employees to save for future medical costs, tax-free. Private sector companies figured this out long ago. Even the strongly unionized auto industry has begun to see the value in shifting away from a defined benefit approach to that of a defined contribution.

As an alternative to offering an open-ended legacy promise of a defined benefit healthcare plan, consider offering a more sustainable product such as a Retiree Medical Savings Account (**"RMSA"**) defined contribution (also called Account-Based) approach to providing retiree medical benefits.

RMSA Characteristics: Employer funds a health reimbursement account for each employee that accumulates tax-free during employment and provides tax-free reimbursement for eligible medical expenses and premiums during retirement. (*Think of it as similar to a retirement income plan coupled with a flexible spending account (§125 FSA Plan)).*

Third, offer a multi pronged solution with the ultimate goal of sunsetting the defined benefit promise and shifting toward a defined contribution plan. Think of it this way; by offering new or future employees a defined contribution program only, mortality will eventually solve the GASB 45 issue for the employer, albeit slowly.

With this approach an employer basically breaks up the group by demographics (e.g., date of hire, years of service, etc.) An employer may, for example, offer employees 50 years or older (those nearing retirement and counting on a promised defined benefit) the same defined benefit plan they are promised today. Typically employers do this for one main reason; this group simply doesn't have enough time to accumulate meaningful assets for future healthcare expenses. Next, for those employees between the ages of 35-50 (ones that still have plenty of time to save) an employer may offer some type of a hybrid plan; one that includes both a defined benefit and a defined contribution. Lastly, for those employees 35 and under, the health benefits could be 100% defined contribution. This may seem aggressive but younger workers are generally eager to take cash today vs. a promise to pay tomorrow. This is a generational mindset. Ask most 30 year olds if they believe entitlement programs like Medicare and Social Security will be around for them at retirement and you will often hear a resounding NO! But, offer this generation money today that they can invest and use for healthcare down the road and they will happily snap it up!

Fourth, offer some type of consumer-directed health plan. The underlying concept behind consumer-driven healthcare is employee engagement. Consumer-directed health plans ("CDHPs") are typically a combination of a high-deductible medical insurance policy coupled with a health care savings vehicle. These savings vehicles can be accessed during the employee's working years to pay for eligible medical care expenses or the account assets can roll-over each year and compound tax-free over time, allowing consumers to efficiently save for future medical expenses. Two significant legislative actions allow for these new CDHP program structures:

- Health Reimbursement Arrangements (HRAs), created by IRS guidance in June of 2002

- Health Savings Accounts (HSAs), which were created as part of the Medicare Prescription Drug, Improvement, and Modernization Act of 2003.

These legislative actions were designed to encourage market growth by allowing tax relief for employers and employees who participate in these programs.

How do Consumer Directed Health Plans ("CDHPs") Work?

The underlying medical plan is generally a "high-deductible health plan" (HDHP) that provides 100 percent coverage for preventive care services such as annual physicals, mammograms, immunizations, and well-child care. Given the higher deductible, these plans are typically less costly than current co-payment type medical plans. Therefore, the premium savings generated by moving to a HDHP can be used to fund some type of health care savings account for each participant. Contributions to the account are made on a pre-taxed basis, any interest earned on the account is typically tax free and in many instances distributions for the account are not taxed. Depending on how the plan is set up contributions can be either employer-funded, employee-funded, or funded by both the employer and the employee[19]. Unused account balances can roll-over from year-to-year providing consumers with financial incentives to make wiser choices in seeking medical care services.

Plan design will dictate at what time funds can be accessed. For example, account holders may have access to their accounts to pay for any qualified pre-retirement and/or post-retirement medical, dental, or vision out-of-pocket expenses allowed by the IRS (deductibles, co-payments, co-insurance, uninsured expenses, etc.), *plus* post-retirement insurance premiums for medical, dental, vision, qualified long-term care premiums, Medicare Part B premiums, Medicare Part D premiums, and Medicare supplement insurance plan premiums.[20] Reimbursements of expenses during active employment as well as after retirement are tax-free to the consumer. Health care savings plans are the only vehicles that allow tax-free reimbursement of post-retirement insurance premiums and expenses.

Having employees enroll in a high-deductible medical plan has a direct effect on the unfunded actuarial accrued liability ("UAAL") of the employer. Since actuaries base future liabilities on the today's healthcare premium cost, any current reduction on premium has a leveraging effective due to compounding.

Source: America's VEBA Solution (a service mark of Genesis Employee Benefits company)

19   Only HSAs allow employee contributions
20   Medicare supplement insurance plan premiums are only reimbursable through an HRA

What about Government subsidies in the future?

According the U.S. Government Accountability Office (GAO), by 2020, the number of individuals in the 55 to 65 age group is projected to increase by 75% and, by 2030, those over age 65 are expected to double, creating the largest percentage of the U.S. population in retirement in America's history.

The Office of the Actuary in the Centers for Medicare & Medicaid Services (CMS) reports that Medicare is fiscally unsustainable as currently constructed. The Hospital Insurance Trust Fund, which provides funding for Medicare Part A, is expected to experience a growing annual cash deficit in 2019, just two years after Social Security outlays are expected to exceed tax revenues in 2017.

The prospect of additional Government subsidization in the years ahead seems unlikely given the current financial state of Medicare and Social Security.

What can be done?

With Medicare available at age 65, there is some comfort in knowing that a subsidized, or pre-funded, form of insurance coverage exists. However, there are large financial "gaps" in Medicare coverage. These gaps include significant cost-sharing provisions (deductibles and coinsurance). Another gap is Medicare Parts B and D premiums, which are the responsibility of the participant. Currently, this collective financial gap accounts for 45% of total health care costs, or approximately $12,885 per year per couple, according to the GAO.

Source: America's VEBA Solution (a service mark of Genesis Employee Benefits company)

Fifth, pre-fund defined benefit OPEBs to utilize the advantages of a higher long-term discount rate during actuarial valuation. Pre-funding can significantly reduce the overall liability. Using the legally-allowed higher discount rates assigned by a qualified actuary can lower the "value" of the liability, and not by a trivial amount. Using the current pay-as-you-go funding rate of 4.5 percent, California's obligation to its state workers is a whopping $47.88 billion in actuarial accrued liability. By pre-funding at a higher rate of return (discount rate) of 7.75 percent reduces the actuarial accrued liability to $31.28 billion, a 35%

savings. Typically, these higher rates of expected return are produced in a professional managed portfolio with the same risk parameters a pension fund might assume. This is further explored in the chapters to follow on establishing an asset allocation and investment policy.

As described in Figure 9.2, only assets segregated in a trust exclusively for the purpose of providing the non-pension retiree benefits are counted toward a qualified OPEB trust as "separate and apart." The funds cannot revert back to the employer during times of surplus, as in the case of many corporate pensions. There are two common trusts, *IRC Section 501(c)(9) VEBA Trust* and *Section 115 Governmental Trust*. The *IRC Section 501(c) (9) VEBA Trust*, formed in 1928, is a separate tax-exempt entity originally created to protect healthcare benefits promised to railway workers. This structure with its long established history is a popular choice of corporations and governments alike. IRS approval is a simple process and requires a nominal filling fee. The *Section 115 Governmental Trust* is an integral part of government or the government code section that makes governments tax exempt. Section 115 trusts require member entities must have "substantial control" and "substantial financial involvement." Because of this, there is concern that these trusts might not meet the "separate and apart" requirements for a GASB OPEB funding since assets could technically revert back to the employer. A private letter ruling is recommended to earn IRS approval, which can cost tens of thousands of dollars in legal costs. Additional investment restrictions may apply if funds remain under limited public investment policies.

Figure 9.2: GASB 43 Trust Rule

A GASB qualified trust or equivalent arrangement must meet the criteria established in GASB Statement 43:

a) Employer contributions to the plan are irrevocable

b) Plan assets are dedicated to providing benefits to their retirees and their beneficiaries in accordance with the terms of the plan

c) Plan assets are legally protected from creditors of the employer(s) or the plan administrator

---

Sixth, explore other funding sources such as issuing OPEB obligation bonds to fund all or a portion of the Actuarial Accrued Liability.

Raising cash by issuing bonds today can simultaneously achieve several goals at once. First, today's interest rates are historically low and credit spreads are narrowing, allowing state and local governments to take advantage of lower interest rates than they might encounter at a later date with higher risk premiums. As governments become more and more strapped for cash going forward, it may only get harder to direct funds toward this goal. Governments have every incentive to issue bonds now, before their contemporaries eventually flood the market with new supply and cause yields to rise. Secondly, when the raised funds are placed into a healthcare trust, state and local governments will be able to take advantage of the preferable long-term discount rate, which reduces the liability.

Conclusions: Utilizing the steps outlined in this chapter, state and local governments can get their OPEB liabilities under control. There is no magic bullet that will make the promises made to retiring Baby Boomers disappear. But by taking these steps, the problem can be made more manageable. Failure to act may result in severe financial distress for all levels of government, resulting in reduced services, higher taxes down the road, and legions of disappointed voters with which to contend.

The huge transfer of intergenerational wealth predicted for Baby Boomers as they inherit the estates of frugal seniors may be hitting a big obstacle—the cost of health care for aging seniors, who are living longer than ever before. A 65-year-old couple retiring in 2008 will need about $225,000 to cover medical expenses in retirement, according to a health care cost estimate released by Boston-based Fidelity Investments.

AARP estimates that 9 million Americans needed long-term care in 2006 and projects an increase to 12 million in 2020. Yet, a 2008 AARP study shows that only two in 10 respondents can estimate monthly nursing home costs within plus or minus 20 percent and nearly that same amount admit they don't know. Those numbers haven't moved significantly since 2001 when AARP administered its first long-term care survey.

A 2006 survey by Genworth Financial placed the average cost of a private room in a nursing home at $70,912 a year, a 2 percent increase over 2005. A one-bedroom private unit in an assisted living facility averages $32,394 a year, a 7 percent increase over 2005.

In the AARP survey, 59 percent of respondents mistakenly believe Medicare pays for extended nursing home care, and 52 percent think Medicare covers assisted living costs. In fact, Medicare covers only acute health needs such as heart attack, cancer or a broken hip, not ongoing daily care. Only the very indigent receive assistance for nursing home care, and assisted living isn't covered at all. Neither is medical equipment such as shower rails or chairs, or incontinence supplies.

Bottom line: Caring for your parents and grandparents in their later years can become an economic drain on their finances and your own. Have an open discussion with them and other family members about what preparations they have made and the resources they may have available for their care, such as health insurance, long-term care insurance, disability insurance and savings. Look at worst case scenarios and brain storm possible solutions, which may include a parent living with you or another family member, home care, assisted living, and nursing home care.
Source: Securities America Financial Corporation

Part III: Portfolio Strategies

Building a Durable Plan for an Uncertain Future

Chapter 10: Portfolio Strategies, Part I

This chapter is primarily intended for portfolio managers or for other fiduciaries who are responsible for the assets of others, but the principles covered will be useful to individual investors as well.

In the previous chapters, we laid out a forecast for the economy and stock market, based largely on the demographic work of Harry S. Dent, Jr. Now, we will offer some advice on how to position your assets and those of your clients to best survive and prosper in the decades ahead.

"Indexing" has gained in popularity in recent decades, based on the work of academics such as Jeremy Siegel, the Wharton professor and author of the wildly influential book *Stocks for the Long Run*. For those unfamiliar with the terms, indexing is simply replicating the performance of a benchmark index, such as the Dow Jones Industrial Average or the S&P 500. For most individual investors, this is best done with a mutual fund or Exchange Traded Fund (ETF), though larger institutional investors will find other methods, such as sampling or the use of futures contracts, to be more cost effective.

To be sure, there is a lot to be said for indexing. Most equity mutual fund managers find it difficult to match their respective benchmark over time, let alone beat them, so indexing often results in better performance, lower turnover (and thus lower taxes), and overall lower fees. So, if you can't beat the benchmark, you might as well join it. Of course, there are exceptions. Many actively-managed funds have had great success in adding "Alpha," or returns in excess of the benchmark index, over periods of time. If you are paying the higher internal fund expenses for active management, you should expect your fund manager to add value, and many do an excellent job of this.

Whether you choose to "index" or use actively-managed mutual funds, it generally makes sense to limit your buying and selling churn and allow your strategy to work.

Does this mean that portfolio managers are obsolete? Absolutely not. Portfolio managers have an important role; it just so happens that picking a basket of stocks that "beats the S&P 500" isn't one of them. After all, your client will take little comfort in the fact that your stocks "beat the market" if the market was down 50% and you were "only" down 40%. Let mutual fund managers concern themselves with beating the S&P 500 (or whatever they use as their benchmark). Portfolio managers have a more important role: determining what benchmark or benchmarks to use, given your portfolio objectives and capital market expectations.

For reasons that will be discussed below, portfolio managers have the ability to add the most value as asset allocators or *portfolio strategists*, not stock or bond pickers. As we discuss later in more detail, more than 90% of the differences in investor performance are explained purely by asset allocation decisions. This is where a good portfolio strategist makes all the difference in the world.

Asset Allocation 101

The asset allocation process can be broken down into six steps, applicable equally to individual investors, financial advisers, and even institutional investors.

1. **Define your Goals**

   This is known in the industry as the "Investment Policy Statement." In this section, you define investment goals based on such factors as return needs, time horizon, risk tolerance, and other preferences. We will cover this in much greater detail below.

2. **Determine the Fundamental Direction of the Economy and Markets using Demographics and Market Cycles**

   This is where the economic insights of the previous chapters come into play. For example, based on the HS

Dent Spending Wave, do you expect the economy to be expanding or contracting? Will inflation or deflation be the norm? Are price-earnings ratios expanding or contracting? What can long-term cycles tell you about the likely trend? In this section, you develop your capital market expectations: how should you expect the market and various asset classes to perform?

3. **Determine your Portfolio Strategy**

Based on the investor's goals from #1 and your capital market expectations from #2, how do you allocate the funds in such a way to maximize the return for a given level of risk? You can adopt a strategic allocation with the intention to "buy and hold" until the conditions in #1 or #2 change, or you can adopt a more active strategy using tactical allocation to take advantage of short-term opportunities.

Do you prefer active management within your chosen asset classes or are you content with indexing? What about income distributions? These are all issues to be addressed when formulating a portfolio strategy.

4. **Investment Manager Selection**

Which funds or managers do you want to utilize in executing your strategy? Is one mutual fund better than another? Is one ETF indexing benchmark more appropriate than another? In these cases, it's important to investigate both the manager and his or her fund or company.

5. **Monitor and Rebalance**

Over time, your portfolio positions will deviate from your strategic allocation. To give a simple example, if stocks have an incredible year, stocks will be overweighted in the portfolio relative to, say, bonds or cash. It's important to regularly rebalance the portfolio back to its target allocation. The optimal frequency for rebalancing is a topic often discussed in financial white papers, and there is no simple answer. Every investor's situation is different. Some managers prefer to rebalance at set time intervals while others prefer to rebalance only when the portfolio reaches some critical level of deviation from the target. The method you choose is up to you, but rebalancing once per year is generally sufficient.

It's also important to monitor the investment managers and funds within the portfolio. Perhaps your targeted asset class is performing well, but the manager is not. Sometimes it is necessary to change managers within a given asset class or strategy.

6. Reporting

Finally, there comes a time to measure your strategy's success. The rule of thumb in the industry is to sit down at least once per year to review your goals and compare them to the actual results. Did the portfolio positions beat their respective benchmark? What about the portfolio as a whole? And most importantly, are you achieving your goals?

The All-Important Investment Policy Statement

At this point, we would like to return to #1, the Investment Policy Statement ("IPS"), and explore that theme a little more in depth. This may seem like meaningless detail at first, but regulators and compliance departments take it seriously—as they should! When a manager is responsible for the assets of another person or institution, they have a serious fiduciary responsibility to manage those assets within guidelines that are suitable to the client. The formality of the IPS makes this much easier and systematic.

The standard IPS formula, the one taught to legions of MBA students and CFA candidates, is as follows. Whether advising an individual, family office, government investment fund, foundation, pension plan, or some other institution, the manager must analyze the following characteristics of the client:

- Return Expectation
- Risk Tolerance

- Time Horizon
- Tax Consequences
- Liquidity Constraints
- Legal Issues
- Unique Circumstances

We'll go over each of these briefly:

Return Expectation and Needs: Here, the portfolio manager or investment advisor may help you determine what rate of return is required to meet your short-term and long-term goals and what return is reasonable to assume based on your tolerance to risk. The portfolio manager or investment advisor may also incorporate his or her capital market expectations into the mix, based on historical statistics or on forward-looking models, such as the Dent demographic models discussed throughout this book. In finance, greater return is expected to come only with greater risk, and this generally holds true.

Risk Tolerance: The portfolio manager or investment advisor may also help you determine how much risk you are willing and able to take, typically (though not always) defined as standard deviation of returns. The refinement of risk tolerance is further determined by assessing the remaining five characteristics below.

Time Horizon: When will you need the money? Are you an elderly widow who needs large income distributions now to meet living expenses? Or a public employee benefits plan, with thousands of employees retiring over the course of several decades? Longer time horizons generally allow for more risk to be taken.

Tax Consequences: Are the funds taxable? Or, are they held by a tax exempt institution such as a government agency, foundation, or held in a tax-deferred account such as a 401k? The tax status can have a big impact on the timing of purchases and sales.

Liquidity Constraints: Do you have immediate need for the funds? Or are the withdrawal needs still years or decades away? This factor is closely related to Time Horizon.

Legal Issues: Sometimes manager discretion is limited by legal requirements that the client funds be invested a certain way or in certain asset classes. Some securities or asset classes may be prohibited for legal reasons. As always, basic levels of professional prudence are required, typically represented by the Prudent Investor Rule, so certain types of institutional accounts also have specific laws that govern manager behavior, such as the Employee Retirement Income Security Act (ERISA).

Unique Circumstances: This is a "catch all" category for special client situations. Perhaps the manager cannot buy tobacco or defense stocks because the client requests "socially responsible" investing. Perhaps the client has large holdings of a single stock that cannot be sold due to family connections to the founder, or perhaps a government fund is required to hold securities from within that state and must adhere to specific maximum time periods and credit ratings.

Putting it to Work

Once the manager determines the basic risk tolerance and return requirements for the client, it is time to select an appropriate portfolio allocation. This means dividing the client's funds among a number of asset classes that together form a portfolio with the expected return and risk characteristics. This is where a portfolio strategist can add real value, and this is where we will focus most of the rest of our portfolio management discussion in the following chapter. We will discuss asset classes and various strategies on combining them to form the best portfolios.

We live in an exciting time to be in the capital markets, but it will also be a dangerous time for those that do not fully understand the changes coming. In the years ahead, there will be asset classes and entire countries best avoided, or at least underweighted. There will also be others that safely grow investors' wealth with minimal risk. We will now take the lessons of conventional asset allocation and apply them in unconventional ways.

Chapter 11: Portfolio Strategies, Part II

The core tenet of modern portfolio theory is diversification. In a nutshell, if you combine any two or more assets with less than perfect correlations, the expected return of your portfolio over time will be the weighted average of the returns of the individual assets in the portfolio. The risk of the portfolio, however, will be *less* than the weighted average risk of individual assets due to the benefits of diversification. This holds true for a simple portfolio of two American stocks like Wal-Mart and Google, a broad index like the S&P 500, or an international portfolio composed of stocks and bonds from around the world.

The Secret to Reducing Risk

Correlation Between Asset Classes					
	Fixed Income	US Large	US Small	Int'l Large	Int'l Small
Fixed Income	1.00	0.25	0.13	-0.04	-0.19
US Large	0.25	1.00	0.77	0.59	0.32
US Small	0.13	0.77	1.00	0.50	0.41
Int'l Large	-0.04	0.59	0.50	1.00	0.82
Int'l Small	-0.19	0.32	0.41	0.82	1.00

Source: Bloomberg

Fixed Income - Lehman Gov't Corp/TR 1973-1991, Bloomberg 3-5 year Gov't Bond 1992-2007

US Large - S&P 500 1973-2007

US Small - DFA US Small Company 1973-1978, Russell 2000 Small Company 1979-2007

Int'l Large - MSCI EAFE 1973-2007

Int'l Small - DFA Int'l Small Company 1973-1996, MSCI EAFE Small 1997-2007

Figure 11.1: The Secret to Reducing Risk

Figure 11.1 is a matrix that lists the correlations between several common asset classes over the past three decades of usable data. As an example, find the row/column intersection of U.S. Large Caps and International Large Caps. The chart reveals a correlation of 0.59, meaning (in layman's terms) that the two move together about 60% of the time (a statistician would get more technical, but this definition is sufficient for our purposes). So, U.S. and international stocks generally move in the same direction, though certainly not in lockstep. Now, compare the correlation between Fixed Income and International Small Cap. It's a negative 0.19, meaning that the two tend to move in opposite directions. (As a point of reference, 1.0 is perfect, lockstep correlation in which the two assets move together; -1.0 is perfect negative correlation, meaning they move in exact opposite directions; 0.0 is no discernable correlation at all, either positive or negative, meaning that the two assets move completely independently of each other).

Obviously, the lower the correlation between two assets or asset classes, the more diversification benefits you get. This means less portfolio volatility for a given level of return. There are certain common risk factors that affect all risky assets, such as interest rates and country-specific risk premia. So, it's very difficult to find two stocks or asset classes that truly have zero correlation. But as we discussed, any correlation less than 1.0 is beneficial to the portfolio!

So, now that we have a basic understanding of correlation, the next essential concept is that of the asset class.

An Introduction to Asset Classes… and What to do With Them!

In figure 11.1, we list the correlations between asset classes. The next logical question is "what constitutes an asset class?"

An asset class is any group of assets that share similar risk and return characteristics. For example, bonds are debt instruments that pay interest, whereas stocks represent actual ownership in an underlying company. The primary factors that affect bond prices are the underlying credit worthiness of the issuer, term or structure and maturity of the security, and current prevailing market rates. Stock valuation is far more complex, incorporating interest rates but also uncertain assumptions about growth, profitability, and even business regulation.

Bonds obviously have much different characteristics than stocks, but both can be further broken down into sub-classes. This is because some bonds behave very differently than other bonds, and the same is true for stocks. For example, if the Federal Reserve announces a surprise interest rate cut, not all bonds or stocks react the same way. Some bond rise in price more than others, and the same goes for stocks. As another example, after the terrorist attacks on September 11, 2001 all U.S. stocks fell in price. But stocks of airlines fell much harder, for obvious reasons. In contrast, most classes of bonds actually *rose* in price after the attacks.

As a general rule, standard U.S. government bonds behave very differently than U.S. government bonds with an inflation adjustment (called "TIPS," for Treasury Inflation Protected Securities). And both behave differently across maturities. In other words, a one-year bond has much different risk and return characteristics than a 30-year bond, which tends to be much more volatile. And naturally, bonds with embedded options, junk bonds, and bonds denominated in foreign currencies add their own unique wrinkles to the mix.

Similarly, large-cap stocks behave much differently than small-cap stocks, and various sectors (such as financials, energy, tech, etc.) have varying correlations with one another. You can combine these sectors in virtually unlimited ways, depending on what your capital market expectations and risk tolerance are. This is a theme that we will expand upon in the next chapter on international and sector diversification. And if you like perusing a lot of data, see the appendix section for performance history of various market indexes and asset allocation models.

You have no doubt heard of "asset allocation," and we touched on it briefly in the last chapter. But you may not have a good grasp of what it is and why it is important. Asset allocation is the science (or perhaps art) of arranging asset classes in such a way that minimizes portfolio risk for a given level of return, within the context of your Investment Policy Statement.

A 1991 study concluded that ***asset allocation policy explained a full 91% of the differences in returns among investors*** (Figure 11.2). In contrast, market timing and security selection explained 2% and 5%, respectively. Picking the next Google or Microsoft is not essential to achieving your portfolio goals, but proper distribution of your monies across asset classes clearly is. You may do well picking individual stocks, but your asset allocation will be responsible for the lion's share of your returns.

The Importance of Asset Allocation

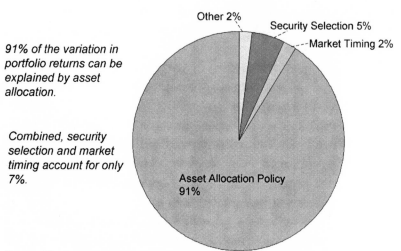

91% of the variation in portfolio returns can be explained by asset allocation.

Combined, security selection and market timing account for only 7%.

Figure 11.2: The Importance of Asset Allocation

So, now that we have established the importance of allocation, let us now explore several common asset classes and give our best assessment of their future prospects.

U.S. Equities

Under most market conditions, U.S. equities should be the backbone of most investors' portfolios, whether they are purchased directly or via mutual funds and ETFs. The stock market remains the most effective way to capture the spectacular growth of the American economy, and it is the vehicle that has created the retirement nest eggs for millions of people.

All of this said, there are long periods where U.S. stocks do not make money, especially after adjusting for inflation. The 1930s and 1970s were truly miserable decades for American investors. 2008 was arguably the most brutal year in the history of the stock market. There are times, such as those, when investors would be best served by reducing their exposure to stocks in general and American stocks in particular. As we have mentioned several times throughout this book, Harry Dent's Spending Wave suggests that we may already be in such a time period. Only time will tell how accurate Mr. Dent's forecast proves to be, but we strongly encourage investors to take it seriously. Demographic trends suggest that the primary engine of the American economy, consumer spending, will lose steam over the next decade. We are looking at a decade going forward in which GDP growth should be modest at best, and corporate sales and profits are likely to have growth rates that are disappointing. Under these conditions, it's hard to imagine U.S. stocks performing very well. We recommend that investors take this into account when constructing their capital market expectations and asset allocations. Be prepared to lower your allocation to stocks in general and U.S. stocks in particular. Or, at the very least, consider adopting a tactical rebalancing strategy that enables you to take advantage of bear market rallies without exposing you to the full risk of a buy-and-hold portfolio.

International Equities

If you have an allocation to stocks, then you certainly shouldn't limit yourself to your home country. The United States dominates world capital markets, and this is not going to change any time soon. That said, U.S. stocks comprise only about half of the world's total value today versus two-thirds back in the 1970s, measured by market capitalization. This proportion varies from year to year, as individual country stocks rise at different rates and changes in currency affect the values, but a 50/50 proportion of U.S./non-U.S. is a good estimate for our purposes.

So, if the stocks of different countries are not perfectly correlated (more on that in the next chapter), and U.S. stocks are only half of the world's total, international diversification is a must if you are to get the maximum return for a given level of risk.

The traditional way to diversify internationally for a U.S. investor is to buy a fund that is indexed to the MSCI EAFE ("Morgan Stanley

Capital International Europe, Australia, Far East") Index. But why stop there? Each of the constituent countries within the EAFE all have their own distinct characteristics, and much of the world is not included in the index at all. Emerging markets are left out entirely, and these have been the best performing markets in the world this decade, their 2008 collapse notwithstanding. We'll return to this theme in the next chapter when we explore various country and sector strategies. For the remainder of this chapter, we will focus more on traditional portfolio allocation and will offer several models for investor to use as examples.

A Word on Emerging Markets

Throughout the decade of the 2000s, emerging markets have been all the rage among investors, though most country indices took punishing losses in 2008. Institutional managers had finally managed to forget their painful losses in this sector in the late 1990s and had again started to enthusiastically pour money into every country from China to Chile. Individual investors embraced the sector as well, dumping their hard-earned funds into emerging market mutual funds with an almost reckless abandon. Of course, virtually all of spectacular profits were lost during the credit meltdown and its aftermath. The sector may well recover in the years to come, but with the global economy in such a fragile state it is hard to imagine a return to the euphoria of the bull market.

We would summarize our view as such: if your risk tolerance warrants an allocation to emerging markets, keep it relatively small and keep in mind that bull markets don't last forever. There may or may not be a dotcom-style implosion; only time will tell. But at any rate, do not expect the stellar returns of the past few years to resume overnight. Investors now realize that the higher returns achieved in this sector in recent years came at the "cost" of higher risk.

Wilshire Consulting had some relevant comments on the matter in their 2007 Asset Allocation report:

> Money managers have long supported the view that emerging
> markets should produce returns above the developed EAFE
> markets. Poor returns in the late 1990s combined with emerging

markets' high volatility have however, caused some managers to re-evaluate their position. **In fact, it is important to understand that the historical record on emerging market performance is short and shows mixed results** [Emphasis ours]....

The last three years, however, have seen emerging markets outperform developed equity markets by a wide margin, as measured from the start of the MSCI Emerging Markets Index. This has caused the relative returns for emerging markets to again be superior to those of the developed markets in a similar fashion to that seen in the early 1990's... **[T]his appears to be a cyclical phenomenon and as such, is not a sufficient reason to justify a long-term return premium** [Emphasis ours]....

Wilshire Consulting, among others, has found that emerging markets do not offer superior risk-adjusted returns over the long run. When they boom, they boom. But when they bust, they bust hard, erasing many years' worth of profits, as we saw in 2008. This does *not* mean that they should be avoided entirely, of course. They can and should have a place in most growth-oriented investor portfolios. Investors in emerging markets made fortunes for much of the 2000s. They should simply be reasonable in their assumptions going forward and should not come to view them as a get-rich-quick scheme, as investors did with tech stocks in the 1990s. As Wilshire continues:

> Our research shows that efficient portfolios include a small allocation to emerging markets.... In this framework, emerging stock markets become a risk management or diversification vehicle rather than an asset class that is expected to generate higher long-term returns.

Like all asset classes, emerging markets should be viewed within the context of a total portfolio. And the allocation to emerging markets can and should be adjusted with your capital market assumptions. This means that investors will probably want to keep their allocation to this sector relatively modest and should again consider tactical rebalancing.

Fixed Income

Most portfolios will have some kind of bond component, with the proportion and composition varying by time horizon and risk tolerance. The fixed income universe is enormous, so a comprehensive outlook for all bond sub-classes is much too detailed for this book. We will limit our discussion to the sub-classes most likely to be available to average investors.

The short-term end of the yield curve is dominated by the decisions of the Federal Reserve, and it is impossible to know in advance what the Fed's policy will be. That said, we can offer our best guesses. The economy is in its most precarious state since the Great Depression. We suspect that the Fed will continue with its loose monetary policy well into 2009 and probably far beyond. Rates are likely to remain low for much of the coming decade. They may or may not reach and stay at near 0% as Japanese rates did in the 1990s. That was truly an extraordinary phenomenon, but then, our situation is rather extraordinary too. As we discussed in Chapter 1, we share many of Japan's demographics issues. In any event, we support Dent's view that rates are likely to stay much, much lower than would be considered normal in the next decade.

The same is true for the long-term end of the yield curve. Referring back to Chapter 3, we see inflationary pressures falling in the next decade. And as 2008 proved, outright deflation cannot be ruled out. Under these conditions, bond yields will fall, meaning that prices will rise. This already happened with Treasury segment of the bond market in 2008. Yields on both the 10-year and the 30-year Treasury strongly suggested that bond investors foresaw deflation going forward. Interestingly, it did not happen with non-Treasury debt, as we see reflected in the spreads between Treasury and Corporate (black line) and Municipal (gray line) securities in Figure 11.3.

Spreads of 10 Year Corporate and Municipal Bond Yields vs Treasuries 1996 - 2008

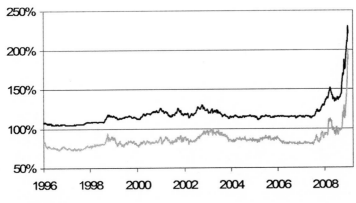

Source: Bloomberg

Figure 11.3: Corporate and Municipal Spreads

During relatively benign times in the economy, investors see little risk in owning the debt of corporations. In 2007, investors were comfortable enough to bid up the price of high-quality corporate bonds to the point where the interest rate was less than 1% higher than Treasuries of comparable duration. Over the past decade, risk premiums had shrunk to levels previously viewed as impossible. Essentially, there *was* no risk premium for most of the mid-2000s, meaning that bond investors took additional risks without a commensurate level of return. Of course, the sub-prime crisis of 2007-2008 sent investors running for quality, and the widening credit spreads in Figure 11.3 were the result, reintroducing vastly higher risk premiums. And again, this was for high-quality bonds. The spread for high-yield "junk" bonds is off the charts.

We believe that high risk premiums are likely to persist for several years to come. Investors are likely to continue to demand a higher yield to compensate for the risk inherent in lower quality assets.

All credit spreads have widened during the credit crunch of 2007-2008, including municipal securities, with tax exempt yields far above comparable treasuries. This has led many state and local agencies to cancel or postpone issuing debt, just when it is needed most.

Bottom line: with the massive re-pricing of the bond sector, investors are being paid to take risk again. Risk-averse investors should continue to have a large portion of their bond holdings in government securities, but they should also make substantial room for the highest-quality corporate bonds and the highest-rated municipal bonds. In this economic environment, there is legitimate credit risk involved when buying non-government debt. But at least investors are being compensated for that risk, which was not the case for most of the 2000s. In constructing bond portfolios, investors should take as much risk as would be fitting given their IPS, though we would suggest limiting that risk to high-grade corporate and municipal bonds. We would still be reluctant to recommend high-yield or emerging market bonds. For that level of risk, equities would be a better investment in our view.

Commodities

It is debatable whether commodities should constitute an asset class for investors. There is no doubt, commodities as a class and individual commodities such as oil or gold as sub-classes have unique risk and return characteristics. They also generally have low correlations to other classes like stocks and bonds. So, at first glance, commodities would appear to be an obvious choice for investor portfolios. Our reservation in recommending them is that, despite the flurry of new mutual funds and ETFs, commodities are not an easy class in which to invest, and there are mechanical problems with most commodity indices.

Few people have the means or the interest in buying gold bricks, barrels of oil, or of filling their backyard with cattle or hogs. For this reason, most investors use futures contracts to gain exposure. Even most commodity index funds use futures rather than the underlying commodity, although notable exceptions include the gold and silver ETFs.

As we discussed in Chapter 6, the rush of investor interest in commodities has distorted the normal workings of the futures markets, with undesirable results for investors. We wrote:

> Investor interest has also contributed to the destruction of the roll yield in several commodities, most notably oil. Without going

into the technical details, it has almost always been possible to earn a passive profit by rolling over oil futures contracts month-to-month. So, by following a passive "buy and hold" strategy with the futures contracts, investors could earn, say, 11-12% on their contracts while the actual oil price only rose, say, 10%. Over time, "total return" commodity indices vastly outperform spot commodity prices. Today, this has been turned upside down. The shear volume of investor interest in commodity futures has forced many (including oil) into contango, meaning that investors are actually losing money every month by rolling their contracts. Much of their profit from the recent spike in the oil price has been eroded, yet investors continue with this strategy, both institutional and individual investors alike.

These shortcomings notwithstanding, commodities may still be a viable asset class for some investors. Our advice is to invest only after understanding the limitations of most investment vehicles in the sector. The discussion in the emerging markets section is also relevant here. Commodity booms do not last forever, and when they bust, they tend to bust hard. Consider the price of oil, which fell from it all-time high of just under $150 per barrel to a recent low in the $40s. Most industrial commodities are also sharply off their lows. A resurgence in global demand, particularly from India and China could again send most commodities higher. But we maintain that the easy money has already been made in this sector, and that the commodity bull market is likely over for years to come. Any future allocation to commodities should be relatively small.

Commodities should be viewed primarily as a diversifier, not a major source of portfolio growth. In the discussion to follow, we will not be including commodities as an asset class.

A Portfolio for Every Investor

In the previous chapter, we explained the stages of the asset allocation decision and the importance of having an Investment Policy Statement. Once an investor (or their advisor) has gone through these processes and determined what the appropriate return and risk expectations are, it's time to actually choose a portfolio model.

In theory, an infinite number of portfolios can be constructed, each ever so slightly different from the others in its risk and return characteristics. In practice, it is generally reasonable to construct three to eight models, give or take, ranging from conservative fixed income to aggressive growth with models such as "growth" or "balanced growth" falling somewhere in the middle. A conservative portfolio will be primarily concerned with preservation of capital, with modest income or capital appreciation as secondary objectives. An aggressive portfolio, in contrast, will be focused almost entirely on capital gains, and will be willing to take substantial risks to achieve this. A conservative portfolio might be appropriate for an elderly retiree or for an investor with an immediate need for cash, whereas an aggressive portfolio might be appropriate for a relatively wealthy or young investor with no immediate needs for the funds. Most investors will fall somewhere in the middle, requiring growth but only at a moderate risk. These are just broad generalizations, of course. The reality will depend on the investor's investment policy statement and on the judgment of the financial advisor.

The next question is, what do we use to construct the models? The truth is, it is really a matter of preference. Some advisors use mutual funds or ETFs, while others use individual stocks or bonds. The "best" option will vary with client circumstances and advisor expertise.

Figure 11.4: "Balanced Growth" Sample Model

US Large Stock
15% large growth
13% large value

International Stock
6% large growth
7% large value
7% emerging growth

US Small Stock
7% small growth
8% small value
4% emerging growth

Bond
10% limited term govt. (1-3yr duration)
7% govt. bonds
5% all bond (diversified high grade)
2% corporate (high grade)
1% corporate (high yield)

US Mid Stock
8% mid blend (growth/value)

Source: RCM Robinson Capital Management

To give an example of this process in action, consider Figure 11.4. This is a sample model used by RCM Robinson Capital Management. In this "Balanced Growth" model, we have created an asset allocation structure that may be appropriate for a long-term investor, health benefit trust or pension portfolio. It is designed for use in an expanding economy, and weighted to take advantage of improving U.S. markets. Of course, having the ability to shift your asset allocation policy is an absolute necessity when facing changing fundamental conditions.

Hence, figure 11.5 offers a look at a portfolio designed for the conservative investor, one with a low risk tolerance and/or a short-term time horizon. This "Capital Preservation" model may also be best suited for the beginning phase of the potentially great economic downshift that we described in Part 1 of this book. As always, we have to offer the standard disclaimer: past performance is no guarantee of future returns. In this case, we are not recommending any of these portfolios. Our objective is merely to use these sample portfolios as an example of asset allocation in action.

Figure 11.5: "Capital Preservation" Sample Model

US Large Stock

3% large growth

5% large value

International Stock

2% large growth

4% large value

0% emerging growth

US Small Stock

0% small growth

2% small value

0% emerging growth

Bond

27% limited term govt. (1-3yr duration)

44% govt. bonds (3-10yr duration)

3% all bond (diversified high grade)

10% corporate (high grade)

US Mid Stock

0% mid blend (growth/value)

0% corporate (high yield)

Source: RCM Robinson Capital Management

Putting it All Together

In this chapter and in Chapter 10, we are not "reinventing the wheel." We are simply laying out the traditional tenets of portfolio management, defining what risks and returns an investor requires and attempting to match them with an appropriate portfolio.

In the next chapter, we cover more advanced portfolio management strategies and tactics, such as making dedicated allocations to specific foreign countries and industrial sectors. These options will not be available to all investors or advisers in their real-life investing, as their portfolio choices are often limited. But for those with flexibility the principles in Chapter 12 should be extremely valuable.

Chapter 12: International and Sector Diversification

In the previous chapter, we reviewed the basics of portfolio theory and examined various strategies for the years ahead. But in this age of mass communications, the world has gotten a lot smaller and a lot "flatter" in Thomas Friedman's words, and investors have started to look beyond their own borders in greater and greater numbers.

This brings up a fair question: In this age of globalization, is there really much benefit to international diversification? In the subprime lending crisis of 2007-2008, virtually all world stock markets fell in unison. Is there any point in diversifying if everything ends up crashing together anyway?

The short answer is an enthusiastic "Yes!"

While correlations tend to get very tight during extreme crashes, these events tend to be rare and generally do not last very long. And when they end, the pre-existing trends tend to reassert themselves, or entirely new trends develop. At any rate, the period of tight correlation is short-lived.

Even as world capital markets become more and more integrated in this age of globalization, stock returns still vary wildly across countries, even countries with similar living standards and industrial structure. Consider this excerpt from Yale professor K. Geert Rouwenhorst, a foremost expert in international finance:

> One of the most surprising empirical regularities in international equity markets is the low correlation among country portfolio returns. For example, between 1970 and 1998, the average correlation between the MSCI index returns of Japan and the United States has been 0.25 [25%], and the correlation between the United Kingdom and the United States 0.50.... By comparison, the correlation between two random portfolios

obtained by splitting the S&P 500 into halves exceeds 0.99. (Rouwenhorst 1998)

This means that two randomly selected halves of the S&P 500 would move in virtual lockstep with each other, despite having none of their stock positions in common. Clearly, country-wide factors affect stock returns, as company or industry factors could not explain such a tight correlation.

International Diversification

As Dr. Rouwenhorst has explained, foreign markets are largely not correlated with each other. Rouwenhorst and his collaborator Heston first explored this topic in their 1994 paper "Does Industrial Structure Explain the Benefits of International Diversification?" in which the authors compared the stock and bond returns of the countries within the Eurozone, or its predecessor the EMU. Even in this tightly integrated region, the authors concluded that the low correlation between country stock indices is almost completely due to country-specific sources and not the industrial makeup of the market. For example, Italy did not lag Spain because Italy had, say, more banks and less manufacturing. There were other factors within the countries that caused the difference. Rouwenhorst confirmed this finding in his 1998 paper "European Equity Markets and the EMU."

And what might those differences be? Traditional economics might suggest that government regulation and fiscal policy were responsible, or perhaps cultural or behavioral factors, but we shouldn't overlook the role of demographics. To give a simplistic example, a chain of toy stores will be more successful is a country full of children than in a country full of middle-aged empty nesters. And naturally, if it makes sense for a single company, the same principle can be applied to the market as a whole. This is the basis of Harry Dent's spending wave from Chapter 1. Perhaps we cannot time every bend and twist in the market, but we can certainly use the model to target countries that are most likely to have booming economies and strong corporate sales and earnings growth due to their demographic trends. We can also underweight or eliminate from our portfolios entirely those countries with negative demographic trends.

Sector Strategies

What is true of countries is also true of sectors within a country, of course. Country factors still dominate, but factors specific to particular industries and sub-industries have a significant impact on securities prices as well.

As we explained in Chapter 11, an asset class is any group of assets with similar characteristics that tend to move together with a high degree of correlation. Among stocks, subclasses exhibit what Chan, Lakonishok, and Swaminathan call "homogeneity in terms of coincidence in stock price movements."

When the Dow Jones Industrial Average or the S&P 500 rise or fall, not all of the component stocks move in the same direction or to the same degree. Some stocks rise, some stocks fall. There are also days when, say, the Nasdaq rises but the Dow falls, or vice versa. The key here is that various groupings of stocks tend to exhibit very different price movements than others.

The question becomes, of course, how do you divide the stocks into homogeneous groups? What constitutes a group? There are differing schools of thought here. Some analysts assign groupings based on fundamental factors such as price/earnings ratio, price/book ratio, or market capitalization. Others use quantitative models that group together stocks based on "statistical clustering," assigning groupings based on historical correlations rather than economic factors.

But as Professors Chan, Lakonishok, and Swaminathan explain in their 2007 paper "Industry Classification and Return Comovement":

> Perhaps the most popular method of establishing sets of economically similar stocks is to follow their industry affiliations. Numerous academic studies provide evidence that industry influences capture a large portion of the extra-market correlations in stock return.... [i.e. returns not explained by the movement of, say, the S&P 500].

Using industry SIC codes, the authors found that industry factors were extremely influential, and the more specific and narrow the SIC classification, the more highly correlated the stocks within the class. We will spare you the technical details of the paper, but suffice it to say, the industrial sector composition of a stock portfolio makes a big difference to performance.

Of course, you already know this. Investors that had large allocations to tech in the 1990s vastly outperformed their peers. These same investors also vastly *under*performed their peers if they held on to those tech shares during the gut-wrenching bear market of 2000-2002. Today, investors heavily allocated to energy and materials are crushing their contemporaries.

This is where the Dent demographic analysis comes in handy. We know that the Baby Boomer generation is aging. An obvious sector to explore would be healthcare, of course. But within the healthcare sector, a further breakdown into subsectors can be useful. For example, companies specializing in pediatric medicine could largely be avoided. The Boomers are well past their peak child-bearing years, and their children are not quite to that stage themselves. Likewise, it may be a bit early to be heavily investing in nursing homes. After all, the Boomers aren't *that* old yet. But they are old enough to be suffering from obesity and diabetes, for example. And all of those vain Boomers who were never quite ready to "grow up" in their 30s and 40s are not quite ready to "grow old" in their 50s and 60s. Cosmetic surgery should be a booming business in the years to come.

We are not offering this as specific investment advice, of course. But we do encourage investors to incorporate this kind of thinking into their asset allocation process. By dividing and subdividing the universe of stocks into distinct asset classes and subclasses, investors can pinpoint stock exposure to the sectors that are most likely to thrive in a given economic environment. Demographics should be a big part of the investment thought process, if not the single biggest.

What About Stock Picking?

With all of this talk of sectors and subsectors, it's fair to ask: is there any point to stock picking? The short answer is "yes," but it's important to keep things in perspective. Picking stocks can add real value, whether it is done by an individual investor or by a professional fund manager, but stock picking should always be done within the context of an asset allocation. Remember, as we discussed in the previous chapter, asset allocation explains 91% of investor excess returns.

In building a portfolio, a "top down" approach is generally appropriate. At the highest level, you must decide how much exposure to have to stocks and to which countries. Once the country allocations have been selected, the next step is determining what weight to give to each industrial sector (or market cap sector, or whatever other subdivision selected).

After selecting the country and sector weights, it is then safe to choose stocks. For example, if you decide to be invested in American pharmaceuticals, you may believe that Merck is a better value than Pfizer, or vice versa. But again—and we cannot emphasize this enough—the key to effectively building and protecting wealth in the capital markets is formulating an appropriate asset allocation that takes into account:

1. Long-term economic trends based on the principles of Part 1 of this book

2. A diversified portfolio properly allocated to countries and sectors to take advantage of the long-term trends while avoiding the major pitfalls.

Of course, there are no guarantees in this business. As every investment manager is apt at disclaiming, "past performance is no guarantee of future results." Still, by utilizing the tools we outline, investors can maximize their chances for success and substantially reduce their risks.

Unfortunately, it is not always possible to do an analysis this elaborate. If the investment options are limited to the five funds in the client's 401k, then in-depth subsector analysis is simply not doable. In this case, the allocation decision is limited to, say, stocks vs. bonds or large cap stocks vs. small cap stocks. If this is the situation, all is not lost. Most investor returns are explained by the return on the overall market, typically quantified by "beta." Simply overweighting or underweighting a stock index like the S&P 500 relative to bonds can potentially be an effective portfolio management tactic if it is done using a model such as the Spending Wave or the now infamous IBES "Fed" model, which compares bond yields to stock earnings yields. However you choose to implement your strategy, first be sure that you *have* a strategy.

Part IV: Demographics in Your Backyard

Understanding the Impact of Demographic Trends in Your Community

Chapter 13: Demographics in Your Backyard, Part I

In this section, we'll take a look at the impact of demographics on state and local economies, with a focus on the largest (and in many ways most challenging) state, California.

We have discussed demographics at length in the previous chapters, expanding on the insights of Harry Dent and the HS Dent Foundation. The fundamental point has been that, more than any other factor, it is age that determines the amount of money a person spends. By extension, you can forecast the general direction of the economy based on the age composition of the country. HS Dent has used the life cycle of the Baby Boomers, the largest generation in U.S. history, to make highly accurate economic predictions about the United States as a whole.

But at the state and local level, the analysis gets considerably more complicated. Nationwide averages may be useful for large-scale businesses, but they do little for the small business owner who depends on local foot traffic. Likewise, knowing the number of children across the country that will be entering kindergarten might be useful to a textbook publisher, but it's not going to be of much use to a local school board. In both cases, local trends are far more important than national. As in real estate, economic decisions are often based on the value of location.

A Zero-Sum Game

As the heading above indicates, at the state and local level population trends can be a zero-sum game. When a Californian moves east to Arizona (and quite a few have), the state has lost an income tax payer and a property tax payer too (or possible a renter, meaning lost corporate income tax from the landlord). Furthermore, California businesses have one fewer customer, and all levels of California government lose that spender's sales tax revenues. Meanwhile, Arizona gains all of these things and prospers.

When the numbers of people entering and leaving a state or city are roughly equal, there is no cause for alarm. This is not at all the case, however. Some states, such as Arizona, Nevada, and (until recently) Florida have benefited from a strong flow of American migrants from other states, in addition to immigrants from abroad. Other states, particularly those in the old industrial "Rust Belt" have had trouble keeping their populations from shrinking. In Michigan, the loss of auto jobs has led to a virtual exodus of humanity. (What infinitesimally small growth the state does have is largely due to natural growth from births slightly exceeding deaths.)

The impact on the areas most affected is easy to understand. The closing of an auto plant and the dislocation of auto workers generally means an out-migration of all of the auxiliary jobs that serviced those auto workers too: everything from dry cleaners to dentists. Given the condition of the Michigan economy, can you imagine opening or expanding a retail store? What about a car dealership (American-made, of course)? It makes little sense to open or expand a local business if your would-be customers are packing up and leaving.

Furthermore, the analysis is more complicated than a simple body count; you must also consider the demographic composition. This is not purely a "quantitative" analysis, but a "qualitative" one as well. The ages and incomes of those who enter and leave are not proportionate to the general population. The people who move tend to be young families of all income ranges who are just beginning their consumer spending life cycle, though high-income professionals and retirees tend to be quite mobile as well. Contrary to popular belief, retirees do not move *en masse*; most tend to stay in the areas in which they had their careers. To put some numbers behind this, the U.S Census Bureau shows that the number of 20-29-year-olds who move exceeds the number of 60-69-year-olds by a full 11 times.

It is the upwardly mobile that pack up and move; it is often the older and less aggressive that stay behind. The areas that receive these go-getter migrants will benefit from a lifetime of earning and spending. The areas that lose these young families lose their future.

This is not abstract conjecture. Think of the last time you took a road trip that took you off of a major interstate freeway. As you were driving down a U.S. or state highway, you probably passed through the central business district of a sleepy, old town that time seemed to forget. Main Street probably looks the same as it did in the 1950s, and this is not a coincidence. When the Eisenhower administration launched the Interstate Highway System, the direction of development in this country was radically changed. Logistics and distribution centers were relocated to take advantage of the faster roads. New gas stations and motels were built to serve the new motorists. Entire new cities sprouted along the paths of the interstates, and the center of business activity shifted away from the old downtowns as a result. Sure, you've heard of Route 66, but its name conjures little more than nostalgia. You certainly would not consider it a major transportation artery today.

The cafés and restaurants in the standard "Middle America" downtown will have plenty of middle-aged and elderly patrons, but there will generally be a conspicuous lack of young workers in their 20s and 30s. Young men and women tend to leave, looking for better opportunities. Without the vitality that young workers bring to an economy, not much changes and the pace of life slows, for better or worse—a classic example of "brain drain."

The popular American author John Steinbeck observed much of this as it was first happening in the 1960s in his classic travel memoir *Travels With Charley*. While Mr. Steinbeck was nostalgic for this "old" America, we are far more pragmatic. Our objective is simply to understand the trends at work and act accordingly to profit from them.

In the case of the interstates, new infrastructure led to new business opportunities, which in turn led to an increase in population, which in turn led to a demand for new infrastructure and business…and the virtuous cycle continued. In contrast, when other cities were "left behind" by the Interstate Highway System, they have generally stagnated and in some cases even declined. A very similar situation occurred during the railroad boom of the late 1800s. Towns in the path of the railroad boomed; towns that were bypassed often withered and faded from memory. Similarly, cities in more recent decades that have invested in major international airports in recent decades—such as Dallas or Atlanta—have grown far faster than those that did not—such as Memphis or Mobile.

Follow the Money

So what does any of this have to do with the plight of cities, counties and states today?   In discussing planes, trains, and automobiles, our objective is not to convince you of the economic benefits of transportation infrastructure. Infrastructure is simply a means to an end, and the end, in our analysis, is population movements. The areas that attract consumers and businesses prosper, and those that do not wither and stagnate. As taxpayers, civil servants, employees, employers, and investors, understanding these trends is critical to our wellbeing. Consider the following except from the *Economist*:

> America as a whole is growing briskly. Between 2000 and 2006 its population swelled by 6.4%, according to the Census Bureau. Yet the expansion has passed many areas by. **Two-fifths of all counties are shrinking** [Emphasis Robinson and Sizemore]. In general, people are moving to places that are warm, mountainous or suburban. They are leaving many rural areas, with the most relentless decline in a broad band stretching from western Texas to North Dakota. In parts, the Great Plains are more sparsely populated now than they were in the late 19th century, when the government declared them to be deserted....
>
> The population of the Great Plains teeters on this shrinking agricultural base. While much of Colorado grew, Cheyenne County shrank every year between 2000 and 2006, when it lost more than 300 people. **Children are disappearing even more quickly** [Emphasis Robinson and Sizemore]. Ten years ago 495 pupils enrolled in the county's public schools; this year 320 did. In Kit Carson, the second-biggest settlement, the school enrolled just four teenagers in the tenth grade. Shops and houses nearby are already boarded up. If the school were to close, there would be little reason for the town to exist at all.[21]

Much of rural America is in the midst of a depopulation spiral

---

21   "The Great Plains Drain." *The Economist.* January 19, 2008

from which it is unlikely to recover. The article goes on to say that local leaders have virtually given up on trying to attract new migrants and have instead focused on managing the decline in such a way as to make life as bearable as possible for those that remain. Some academics have even proposed abandoning large swathes of land altogether to create grazing grounds for wild buffalo!

Clearly, these are extreme cases. And if you are reading this book, chances are good that you do not live in one of these declining rural areas. Still, the fundamental message stands. Prosperity and population changes are inseparably linked.

Migration Trends Re-Drawing the Map

Understanding the type of migrant that an area attracts is significant as well. A high-income, middle-aged "power" couple will contribute far more to a local economy than an elderly couple surviving on social security or a young immigrant family struggling to survive in a new country. So, in analyzing the movement of people, it is also important to determine who exactly is moving. Interestingly, the demographic trends that are busily creating the boom (and bust) towns of tomorrow appear to transcend race and income. A trend that has been obvious since the end of World War II has been that of "white flight," in which middle-class Caucasian families have left urban centers and older suburbs in favor of new, more affluent, and more ethnically homogenous suburban and exurban areas. The areas they left behind were often filled with recent immigrants and less-mobile African Americans and Latinos, two groups who were thought to have not benefited as much from the prosperity of the Information Age. The result was de facto "ghettoization" in which minorities were effectively trapped in ethnic enclaves and excluded from broader society, either by choice or by exclusion. Fortunately, this pattern appears to be reversing in recent years.

In a separate article, the *Economist* describes the migration patterns of African Americans in California:

> Between 2000 and 2006, the black population of Victorville and Apple Valley swelled from 11,900 to 24,500. Two hours' drive from central Los Angeles and surrounded by Joshua trees, it is

an improbable black haven.... Yet Victorville is typical. Other sprawling exurbs, such as Palmdale and Lancaster, are also seeing an influx of blacks looking for cheaper housing and safer streets. They reveal a dramatic shift in southern California's population, and provide clues to how America is changing.

Victorville's gain is Los Angeles's loss [Emphasis Robinson and Sizemore]. Since 1990 the city's black population has dropped by a quarter, from 488,000 to 364,000, even as the overall number of residents rose....

These trends are not limited to Los Angeles. Similar patterns have emerged in other American cities as well, as a wave of urban redevelopment has raised the property values in formerly depressed areas. As the *Economist* continues,

A similar drift is evident in northern California, where blacks are leaving the Bay Area for inland spots such as Stockton and Sacramento.... A big reason is immigration. New arrivals from Latin America and Asia have pushed up rents in the metropolis. Until recently they pushed up house prices, too, benefiting the roughly 40% of black householders in south-central Los Angeles who own property. They could afford to move on.[22]

A similar situation has occurred among Latinos, both recent immigrants and native-born. Historically, the American Latino population has been concentrated in the Southwest border states, between California and Texas. Now, Mexican supermarkets can be found in medium-sized cities and towns in North Carolina and Spanish can be heard in construction sites across the Deep South, an area that is traditionally almost exclusively white and black.

Though unfamiliar accents can be somewhat disruptive in traditional areas, and long-time residents are often wary of the newcomers, these trends are positive for the country in general, and they are certainly better than the alternative. As the *Economist* concluded in the first article, "Compared with the consequences of rapid growth, such as traffic jams and illegal immigration, to which so much political energy is devoted, the problems of depopulation can appear intractable."

---

22   "Straight outta Compton," *The Economist*. February 16, 2008

The breaking up of the ethnic enclaves has expanded American mobility to demographic groups who have not enjoyed it in decades, if ever. The last time American blacks moved in such large numbers was during the decades of the World Wars, when northern factories needed additional manpower. The result today should be the same as before: increased social mobility and prosperity for those who move, which should benefit the country as a whole with higher income and spending.

As the *Economist* points out, much of this was made possible by the wealth created in the real estate boom of recent years. As this has ground to a halt, the movement of people will almost definitely slow. Rising anti-immigrant sentiment will also have an impact. But now that the trends are in place, they are not likely to stop altogether. In the chapters ahead, we will explore further the migration trends at work and the implications for the areas most affected.

Chapter 14: Demographics in Your Backyard, Part II

In the previous chapter, we established that the movement of people matters to a local economy. In this chapter, we are going to look at the numbers and also at some of the more qualitative factors involved. In the next chapter, we will actually go city to city within California, drawing conclusions from the local demographic trends.

So, with all of that said, exactly how large are the migration waves of which we speak? The United States is a nation of over 300 million people, and while a relatively small number of Americans leaves the country, an enormous number do decide to pick up and move *within* the country. To fully grasp how big this trend is, consider HS Dent's analysis of the subject:

> The United States is an extraordinarily mobile society, as evidenced by the fact that 45.9% of the population moved between 1995 and 2000. The majority of those moved within the same state, with 24.9% of people moving within the same county and 9.7% moving within the same state to a different county…. The key groups—the ones that cause the booms and busts—are the 8.4% that moved out-of-state and the 2.9% that are immigrants…. Together, these two migration segments create over 2% in regional population shifts per year, which is greater than our current population growth at 1.1% and exceeds our current birth rates at approximately 2.1%. In numbers, out-of-state migrants and immigrants accounted for 22.1 million and 7.5 million, respectively, or 29.6 million people in 5 years (close to 37 million with illegal immigration). Needless to say, the movement of 37 million people creates a major trend for real estate and business growth in the areas to which these people are moving.[23]

23   Dent, Harry. *.Demographics in Motion.* 2006, HS Dent Publishing, 2006

(For a more in-depth study of the macro demographic trends already underway, we highly recommend giving HS Dent's *Demographics in Motion* a read.)

We have now established that people are moving in large numbers and that this will have a big impact on the areas gaining and losing population. The question then becomes: Where are they going? The short answers are "south" and "west." We will return to this theme shortly. But first, we're going to take a big picture look at the root causes of the ongoing migration.

It's a Flat World, After All

One of the major trends of the past hundred and fifty years has been the shifting of the U.S. population from rural to urban and suburban areas. As agriculture modernized and required less human labor, workers migrated to the cities to take the new jobs created by industrialization, causing major metropolitan areas to grow at the expense of small and medium-sized towns. In the post-war, automobile-dominated era, populations shifted again, from urban centers to suburban satellite cities. Over most of this time period, growth was most concentrated in what we now call the "Rust Belt" and later in California as well. The highly industrialized parts of the country did a phenomenal job of lifting generations of Americans out of rural and working-class poverty and into the respectable middle classes. Unfortunately, in the process, these areas have become high-regulation, high-tax, and high-cost-of-living leviathans.

Since the 1970s, the American economy has been transformed again. The economy has evolved into a "post industrial" system dominated by the service sector. Over the past decade, this process has been greatly accelerated by what Thomas Freedman calls the "flattening" of the world, made possible by free trade, globalization, and the democratization of communications and information technology.[24] The result has been that many of the traditional centers of industry and population have lost the advantages that justified their higher costs.

To illustrate with a simple example, let us compare an "old economy" industry like auto manufacturing with a "new economy" industry like software development. An auto parts manufacturer would find it

---

24   We highly recommend Friedman's 2005 book, *The World is Flat.*

advantageous to be located close to their customer, Ford or General Motors. Likewise, both would find it necessary to be located close to major transportation hubs, be they rail junctions or major highways. At every link in the chain, from raw materials to manufacture to transportation, labor unrest is a potential destabilizer that can grind the entire process to a halt. The same is true of government regulators and taxing authorities. In the industrial economy, the wealth generated by capitalism can be (and often is) held hostage by its own inputs.

Compare this to the information economy. Particularly now, in the Internet Age, software code can be produced virtually anywhere and at a marginal cost of production of $0. Software can be copied infinite numbers of times and delivered at virtually no cost via the internet. Microsoft's "supply chain" is also far easier to mange than that of General Motors. A software engineer can pound out code just as easily on a laptop at Starbucks as in an office cubicle, but an assembly line worker does not have that luxury. Likewise, a strike or supply disruption in a supplier's plant can cripple General Motors's production, but Microsoft has no "production," per se. As Vista proved, new releases can be delayed, but sales of existing software are largely unaffected, driven instead by PC sales.

Microsoft's headquarters is in the state of Washington, but it could just as easily be located in Pennsylvania or even Paraguay. Similarly, Amazon.com, the world's premier "new economy" retailer, can theoretically put its headquarters anywhere it wants with no real effect on its operations. Even your two authors had a large degree of freedom in writing this book. Your elder author collaborates with your younger author in Tampa, Florida from across the country in his office in San Francisco, California. Information technology allows your two authors to efficiently author a book while living on opposite sides of the continent!

Furthermore, outside of medicine, most high-value-added services can be performed remotely as well. Your lawyer, accountant, or money manager can serve you from virtually anywhere. Information and entertainment media can be delivered from anywhere via the internet or by mobile phone or satellite technology. Naturally, traditional trade jobs like those of barbers, plumbers and roofers are anchored to the communities of their customers. These jobs are not mobile, but the high-end "growth" jobs often are.

The evolution of our economy into one that is driven primarily by services and information combined with the revolution in information technology and the opening of markets due to globalization have created a world in which both capital and skilled labor are highly mobile. The result is that both tend to go where they are treated best. This is the root cause behind the waves of migration sweeping across the country. People and businesses move because they *can*. Jobs are being created in the low-cost, low-tax states in the South and West as both companies and individuals move to take advantage of the benefits. The influx of newcomers creates new jobs and opportunities for yet more new migrants, and the virtuous cycle continues. Now that we understand the trends in place, let us now follow the migration patterns.

Head West, Young Man! (and South, Too!)

Populations are moving away from the Northeast, Upper Midwest and from the more expensive of the coastal cities and into the Mountain West and Gulf Coast regions. Figure 14.1, courtesy of the HS Dent Foundation, summarizes the major population movements, what Harry Dent calls the "demographic convection current." Starting on the West Coast, we see a pattern of Californians leaving fleeing high taxes and real estate prices and moving into neighboring western states and even as far east as Texas. Texas is also a major recipient of migrants from the Chicagoland / Great Lakes region, as is the Gulf Coast of Florida. Florida itself is an interesting microcosm of national migration trends. The Gulf Coast, including the booming Tampa / St. Petersburg metro area, tend to attract migrants from the Upper Midwest, while the Atlantic coast tends to dominated by migrants from the Eastern seaboard. The Interstate highway system seems to play a role here. I-75 slants diagonally across the county, from Michigan to the Gulf Coast of Florida, eventually cutting across the state and terminating in Miami. I-95 runs along the Atlantic coast, starting in Maine and also terminating in Miami.

Migration Flows

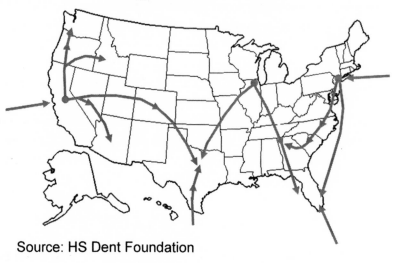

Source: HS Dent Foundation

Figure 14.1: Migration Flows

Another key point, and one that is of particular importance given the debates in the run-up to the 2008 presidential election, is that of immigration. As Figure 14.1 illustrates, California, Texas, South Florida, and New York are major destinations for immigrants, both legal and illegal. There is no shortage of media pundits who are quick to point out the costs of immigration to the areas that receive the immigrants. Lou Dobbs and his contemporaries in the nightly news media will enthusiastically cite statistics of school districts and hospitals nearing the point of bankruptcy due to the cost of servicing immigrants. We are not here to debate those numbers, though we do suspect that there is a fair amount of politically-motivated exaggeration involved.

We prefer to look at the other side of this equation: while the city, county, or state may be shelling out money to build and expand school and hospitals, this money is not "lost." It filters through the local economy. The construction of a new school to service an influx of immigrant children means employment for construction workers and teachers and new business for material suppliers and textbook vendors. More immigrants mean more potential homeowners and renters, which helps to support and increase home values and rental rates for landlords. While a recent immigrant does not have the spending power of a middle-aged doctor or lawyer, he does still require a roof over his head and food in his stomach, and this means higher profits for businesses that cater to these needs. So, while there are certainly costs to large-scale immigration, there are also incredible opportunities. Immigration has declined over the past two years due to a collapse in the construction economy and to stricter enforcement. This has contributed to the downward spiral of falling rents and home prices, and unfortunately, this trend is not highly likely to be reversed.

Without the influx of new immigrants, migration patterns within the United States become much more of a zero-sum game in which one state's gain is another's loss. The same is true of cities and counties within the states.

The 2000s: Region by Region, State by State

Now that we have established the trends, let us put some numbers behind them. Figure 14.2 breaks down the population growth of the United States over the 2000-2007 period. At 1.9% and 2.9% respectively, the Northeast and Midwest regions far underperformed the national average of 6.9%. Meanwhile the South and West vastly outperformed, at 9.8% and 10.5%, respectively. It should be noted that the West posted such incredible gains despite being dragged down by slower-growing California, which, as the largest state in the union by population, completely dominates the region.

Population Growth Rates
% Change 2000-2007

United States	6.9%
Region	
Northeast	1.9%
Midwest	2.9%
South	*9.8%*
West	*10.5%*

Source: US Census Bureau

Figure 14.2: Population Growth Rates, 2000-2007

Over the period, California grew by 7.5%, which is still above the national average. But compared to the gains made by neighboring states, California's look far more modest. As Figure 14.3 illustrates, the growth rates of some of the western states are almost unbelievably high. Nevada and Arizona increased their populations by 27% and 23%, respectively. This makes Texas's growth of "only" 14% look weak in comparison.

Selected states of the Old South did quite well over the period too. North Carolina (12%), Georgia (16%), and Florida (14%) all grew at rates far in excess of the national average, and have enjoyed booming local economies. In terms of population count, these states drew far more people than the Western states, though the Western states are able to grow at faster rates due to their smaller starting populations. It takes fewer people to generate a boom in sparsely-populated Nevada than it does in Florida, the fourth largest state in the union by population!

If current trends continue, the South will indeed "rise again" as a powerful economic and population center. For the reasons discussed in this chapter and in chapter 13, both the South and the West should continue to growth at the expense of the Northeast and the Midwest due to durable advantages of lower taxes and regulation, lower labor and real estate costs, and a more desirable climate.

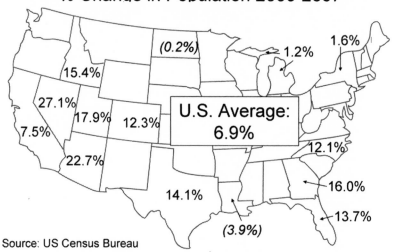

Population Booms and Busts
% Change in Population 2000-2007

Source: US Census Bureau

Figure 14.3: Population Booms and Busts, 2000-2007

Louisiana has thus far been the exception to the rule. Louisiana was losing population even before Hurricane Katrina wreaked havoc on New Orleans and the coast. Unlike her Gulf Coast peers, Louisiana does not have a reputation for being friendly to business, and taxes and the regulatory burden are prohibitively high. The destruction of New Orleans, ironically, has created opportunities for the state. New private investment and a windfall of federal aid will likely perpetuate a mini-boom of sorts. And the port of New Orleans will likely always be a source of income and jobs for the area. But do not expect Toyota or Nissan to open a new factory in Louisiana any time soon, as they have in sister states in the South, and do not expect waves of young white-collar professionals from across the country to flock to the state either. Dallas and Atlanta are far more likely destinations for these highly-sought-after migrants.

The only other state to actually lose population was North Dakota, and this fact has not gone unnoticed by policy makers. The state recently introduced a new program dubbed "Experience ND" with the intention of luring back ex-residents who have left for greener pastures.

It appears that North Dakota is following the example of her neighbor to the south. According to the *Wall Street Journal*,

> South Dakota isn't for everyone. So when the state crafted a program to attract new workers, it targeted people already familiar with its freezing winters and open spaces: the thousands of South Dakotans who leave every year. The result is "Dakota Roots," a year-old job-placement service that matches expatriate South Dakotans with companies that need workers. Dakota Roots is South Dakota's effort to attract former residents. Across the country, in an effort to repopulate declining work forces, several states are going after former residents.[25]

It remains to be seen whether these efforts will bear any fruit. Meanwhile, the leakage of population continues.

Michigan and New York registered gains over the seven-year period, albeit just barely. The slight increase was due to native fertility and certainly not to net migration, which was decidedly negative. The large-population states Ohio and Pennsylvania likewise registered nearly

---

25   Dougherty, Conor. "Ex-Residents Are Gone, But They're Not Forgotten." *Wall Street Journal*, December 26, 2007

negligible growth, at 0.9% and 1.2%, respectively, as did smaller states such as West Virginia and Rhode Island at 0.3% and 0.7%, respectively.

Bucking the trend of their healthier Southern neighbors, Alabama and Mississippi registered mild growth at 4.0 and 2.5%, significantly below the national average of 6.9%. These Gulf states notwithstanding, the trend over this decade has been clear. Net migration has been flowing from the Northeast and upper Midwest into to cheaper and generally more economically libertarian states of the South and West. California, though still growing at slightly above the national average, is not growing as fast as it used to, and its neighboring states in the West are certainly doing their part to pick up the slack.

2007: Region by Region, State by State

Now that we have analyzed the trends over this decade, let us now isolate the changes over the year 2007, the last year for which we have data. In this section, we will see if the trends of the 2000s are perhaps accelerating or decelerating.

In Figure 14.4, we see a continuation of the trends in Figure 14.2. The South and West continue to gain at the expense of the Northeast and Midwest.

Population Growth Rates
% Change 2006-2007

United States	1.0%
Region	
Northeast	0.2%
Midwest	0.4%
South	*1.4%*
West	*1.4%*

Source: US Census Bureau

Figure 14.4: Population Growth Rates, 2006-2007

Moving on to Figure 14.5, we see much of the same as well. North Carolina, Georgia, Texas, and the Western states (excluding California) are growing at more than double the national rate. New York's slow growth continues, and Michigan has actually gone negative. All of these developments are consistent with our arguments throughout this chapter and Chapter 13.

Population Booms and Busts
% Change in Population 2006-2007

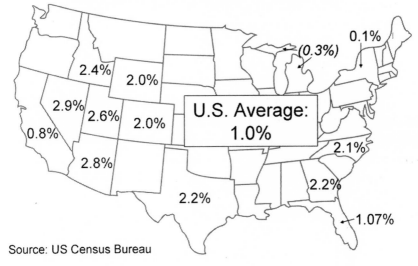

Source: US Census Bureau

Figure 14.5: Population Booms and Busts, 2006-2007

Interestingly, Florida and California have shown marked slowdowns in growth, with Florida dropping to the level of the national average and California dropping slightly below. The reason for these sudden reversals should be quite obvious: California and Florida were the epicenters of the recent housing bubble and burst and where the rampant speculation reached its greatest excesses. Both of these states saw home prices rise to levels that would have been beyond imagination in years past. These two states had some of the highest percentages of exotic and adjustable rate mortgages, as the average homebuyer would have otherwise found the properties to be unaffordable. This exacerbated the housing bubble and made the eventual burst all the more painful.

Home construction and financing had become a disproportionate chunk of the state economy in both California and Florida, and the bursting of the bubble meant a quick evaporation of construction and mortgage jobs. With the largest source of job growth disappearing almost overnight, both domestic migration and immigration from abroad slowed dramatically.

Florida, where the junior of your two authors lives, also saw its lawmakers become increasingly populist with the continued inflation in home prices. Rising home prices meant rising property taxes as well, along with unhappy taxpayers. In an attempt to appease angry voters, the state legislature attempted to soak the "snowbirds and carpetbaggers" by forcing most of the property tax increases onto the shoulders of newcomers to the state. Faced with such a hostile reception, many would-be migrants have opted for Georgia or the Carolinas instead.

Going forward, we believe that Florida will eventually resume growing at above the national average, though at perhaps a slightly lower rate than in past years. As Florida's population continues to increase, it becomes harder and harder to sustain such a torrid growth rate, though we do still believe it will be above the national average. The housing glut will eventually be worked down, and home prices and rental rates will stop their freefall. It may be an ugly couple of years in the meantime, but Florida has several long-term advantages in its favor, such as its absence of a personal income tax and its business-friendly tax and regulatory regime. The cost of living is not as attractive as it used to be, but it is still considerably below that of the Northeast or much of the upper Midwest. Within a few years, Florida will likely be growing at roughly the same rate as Texas.

In the case of California, we are much less optimistic. California does have its advantages, of course. Despite the incredible gains in India, Silicon Valley remains the premier center of innovation in the technology sector. India's Bangalore is becoming a worthy competitor, but for the foreseeable future, Silicon Valley is still where the best and brightest of the tech world congregate, and California will continue to benefit. Of course, during global business recessions, spending on IT infrastructure grinds to a halt, as 2000-2002 proved. Silicon Valley is not immune to booms and busts.

Nor are some of California's other major industries. With federal spending at record levels, with enormous Social Security and Medicare expenses in the pipeline, and with aggressive foreign policy becoming more and more unpopular, we do not see the defense industry enjoying the growth that it has over much of this decade. Given that the United States military budget is already the largest in the world by an order of magnitude, it is unrealistic to expect it to grow much further, especially when new spending on military hardware means less for other programs in an increasingly tight budget.

Even the entertainment industry has its problems. File-sharing programs and online piracy have absolutely decimated the major record labels, and indeed the traditional business model of the entire industry appears to be in terminal decline. Likewise, the film business is suffering from lackluster ticket sales and rampant piracy while major costs such as actor salaries continue to soar. Television is also under pressure, as the internet is becoming more and more of a competitor for eyeballs. Tivo and DVRs have also reduced the effectiveness of traditional advertising, something that affects the profits of both TV studios and advertising agencies, two of California's high-end industries. None of these are positive developments for the state.

We are not suggesting that the film, music, and television industries will disappear, of course. But by now, it is obvious that the business model that has reigned for nearly a century is fast becoming obsolete. These industries will undergo a major restructuring, perhaps even a reinventing. Costs will be cut, which is good for consumers across the country and even across the world. It is potentially bad for California, however, as lower prices mean less sales and income tax revenues for the state and fewer jobs in the industry.

There is more to California than just Silicon Valley and Hollywood, of course. California's economy is larger than most of the economies of Western Europe—measured alone, it would be the seventh largest economy in the world. We do not see the state going the way of Michigan, at least not any time soon. But given the state's high cost of living, high taxes, and the lack of growth in many of its glamour industries, we do not see the state growing at above the national average going forward.

Furthermore, as we explained in the previous chapter, population movements have a qualitative aspect in addition to quantitative. How many young college graduates or recent immigrants from Asia or Latin

America does it take to replace the consumer spending and overall economic impact of one 50-year-old, upper-middle-class professional?

Again, we are not suggesting that California's world-class professionals will leave en masse, to be replaced solely by low-income immigrants and young people. In fact, California continues to attract high-income earners, as we will discuss below. Still, in the economic world, change happens at the margin. If, on average, the people who enter the state have lower income potential than those who leave, over time the state's economic growth rate should slow. In new developments, you will see less Saks Fifth Avenue and more Wal-Mart. This is not an apocalyptic scenario, and for that matter, it is not even as bad as the reality that Michigan and Ohio face. California is a diversified "new economy" state, while Michigan and Ohio are highly dependent on the declining "old economy" of manufacturing.

Our point is simply that the Golden State faces significant obstacles to achieving the growth rates to which it has become accustomed.

In the next chapter, we are going to take a look at some of the city and county-level trends underway in California. Though the state has problems, there will certainly be pockets of opportunity.

Chapter 15: The Golden State

California is in many ways a victim of its own success. Despite being an entire continent away from the other major population and economic centers of the country, California has been a beacon of opportunity for Americans and the world's immigrants alike for over 150 years. But with the incredible prosperity that the state has enjoyed have also come a rising cost of living and a more expansive (and expensive) state bureaucracy. The result has been that government expenditures have outstripped even the Golden State's splendid growth rate, and the state's finances have come under strain.

The *Financial Times* reports that the state of California is running a $14.5 billion budget deficit in 2008, after more than half a decade of solid economic growth.[26] In the same article, the *Times* reports that "Mr. Schwarzenegger has caused a public outcry with a series of measures aimed at curbing spending. The radical proposals include cutting the state's education budget, closing some of its most popular parks and releasing some prison inmates early."

How desperate is the situation? Judging by some of the means California and other states are using to raise revenues these days, the situation appears to be desperate indeed. One of the most noteworthy is the increase in "unclaimed property" being sought by the state. Unclaimed property consists of everything from bank accounts and safe deposit boxes to unredeemed gift cards and uncashed corporate checks that the owners have either forgotten about or abandoned. The *Wall Street Journal* reports that California is one of the states that has modified its unclaimed property laws to, shall we say, more liberally judge what property is, in fact, "unclaimed" and by putting a little less effort into finding the owners. The *Journal* reports that California

---

26   Garrahan, Matthew. "California's Sweeping Budget Cuts Draw Fire," *Financial Times*. January 18, 2008

currently holds more than $5 billion in unclaimed property,[27] some amount of which will eventually find its way back to its rightful owners. Still, if the state manages to keep even half of that total, it would help alleviate the budget deficit that Governor Schwarzenegger is struggling to terminate.

Our goal here is not to criticize the state of California. In truth, it would be downright irresponsible for the state to not make use of any and all sources available, and it's certainly more politically feasible than raising taxes or cutting popular programs. Our point is simply this: If state officials are already resorting to seizing unused gift certificates and uncashed checks to make ends meet, then the fiscal outlook is grim. For reasons discussed throughout this book, from the demographic-based consumer spending downturn to the pension and OPEB funding crisis, state and local governments have very difficult jobs in front of them, and they are not going to get easier any time in the foreseeable future.

All of this said, California's news is not all bad. While State and some local agencies' finances may be currently challenged, private sector trends are still largely positive in the Golden State. Providing evidence of this, the California Department of Finance compiled an excellent demographic analysis based on the 2000 census[28]. By now, some of its findings are getting a bit dated, and we will certainly use more current data in our county-by-county analysis later in this chapter. Still, much of the report is still relevant and consistent with current trends. The state found that,

- Approximately half of the California population moved in the years 1995-2000

- Of these movers, 62% moved within the same county, 20% moved to a different county within California, 9% moved from another state, and another 9% moved from outside the country. The 38% that moved from outside of their existing counties are the ones with the greatest impact.

---

27   Thurm, Scott and Pui-Wing Tam. "States Scooping Up Assets From Millions of Americans," *Wall Street Journal*. February 4, 2008

28   State of California, Department of Finance, *They Moved and Went Where: California's Migration Flow, 1995-2000:* Sacramento, California. June 2007

• Approximately 2.2 million people moved out of California to other states, compared to 1.4 million who moved to California from other states. Another 1.4 million immigrants moved to California from abroad, for a net gain of 652,122.

• Mobility appears to be spread across racial lines, with percentages of Whites, Asians, Blacks, and Hispanics moving at 48%, 50%, 53%, and 54%, respectively.

• Among domestic migrants, California appears to be getting richer through net migration of higher-income Americans, though this is partially neutralized by less affluent immigrants. Overall, among domestic migrants, California had substantial net inflows in the $100,000+ income range and substantial net outflows of all lower income groups. This supports the standard view that younger, less affluent Californians are leaving for better opportunities and lower costs of living in neighboring states and are being replaced by a combination of higher-income professionals and lower-income immigrants.

Echoing the findings of HS Dent's "Demographics in Motion" and the *Economist's* "Straight outta Compton," both mentioned in the previous chapter, the state report confirms a "demographic convection current" at work in California's large coastal cities. Native residents are moving out and being replaced by Americans from other states and, more commonly, by immigrants. As an example, between 1995 and 2000, Los Angeles had a net loss of 300,000 to other counties and a further net loss of 268,000 interstate movers. Much of this loss, however, was mitigated by an influx of 466,000 immigrants.

Immigrants still tend to cluster in core urban areas upon entry into the United States, though they do not necessarily stay there. There is no real evidence of permanent "ghettoization" of immigrants or ethnic minorities. In fact, the much-maligned phenomenon of "white flight" is actually a luxury all races, including American-born Hispanics. Consider Figure 15.1.

Domestic Migrants To and From California by Race 1995-2000

	Outflow	%	Inflow	%
White, not Hispanic	1,302,897	59.1%	1,003,615	69.3%
Hispanic or Latino	**505,947**	**23.0%**	**160,374**	**11.1%**
Asian	151,864	6.9%	127,384	8.8%
Black or African American	161,893	7.3%	98,713	6.8%

Source: California Department of Finance

Figure 15.1: Domestic Migrants To and From California by Race

By shear numbers, Whites dominate both interstate inflow and outflow. Interestingly, they make up a higher percentage of the domestic inflow than they do domestic outflow; whites make up 69% of Americans entering the state but only 59% of those leaving. Conversely, native-born Hispanics are leaving California in much larger numbers and as a bigger percentage than those entering. Over half a million Hispanics left California compared to the 160,374 that entered from other states. These statistics do not include immigration from abroad.

County By County

Continuing the theme of the demographic convection current, let's take a look to see which areas have enjoyed the most growth. In this section we will use more recent demographic data covering the 2000 to 2007 period. Figure 15.2 illustrates the county population "winners" that had the fastest growth rates, while Figure 15.3 labels the counties that are showing the most weakness.

Figure 15.2: Fastest Growing California Counties

Population Growth Rates
Fastest Growing California Counties

County	2000	2006	2007	% Change 2000-2007	% Change 2006-2007
Riverside	1,559,046	2,004,174	2,070,315	32.8%	3.3%
Placer	252,233	322,953	329,818	30.8%	2.1%
Kern	665,294	790,246	809,903	21.7%	2.5%
Imperial	143,522	168,979	174,322	21.5%	3.2%
Madera	124,515	146,064	149,916	20.4%	2.6%
Sutter	79,499	92,715	95,516	20.1%	3.0%
Merced	211,228	248,258	252,544	19.6%	1.7%
San Joaquin	568,978	671,115	680,183	19.5%	1.4%
Yuba	60,413	70,053	71,612	18.5%	2.2%
San Bernardino	1,722,343	2,011,404	2,039,467	18.4%	1.4%
Kings	130,057	149,883	153,268	17.8%	2.3%
Tulare	369,630	422,594	430,974	16.6%	2.0%
Yolo	170,096	193,262	197,530	16.1%	2.2%
Colusa	18,916	21,551	21,945	16.0%	1.8%
Stanislaus	451,016	515,660	523,095	16.0%	1.4%
Fresno	804,274	906,365	923,052	14.8%	1.8%
Sacramento	1,233,549	1,396,496	1,415,117	14.7%	1.3%

Source: California Department of Finance

Figure 15.3: Net Migration in California Counties

Population Growth Rates
Slowest Growing California Counties

County	2000	2006	2007	Change 2000-2007	Change 2006-2007
Sierra	3,629	3,464	3,400	(6.3%)	(1.8%)
Inyo	18,193	18,221	18,253	0.3%	0.2%
Plumas	20,712	21,013	20,891	0.9%	(0.6%)
Modoc	9,525	9,690	9,747	2.3%	0.6%
Siskiyou	44,479	45,618	45,695	2.7%	0.2%
Marin	248,176	254,000	256,310	3.3%	0.9%
San Mateo	710,734	726,260	734,453	3.3%	1.1%
Santa Cruz	256,465	262,150	265,183	3.4%	1.2%
Mendocino	86,536	89,264	89,669	3.6%	0.5%
Tuolumne	54,713	56,882	56,910	4.0%	0.0%
Humboldt	126,853	131,876	132,364	4.3%	0.4%
Sonoma	461,462	477,615	482,034	4.5%	0.9%
San Francisco	781,172	806,210	817,537	4.7%	1.4%
Alpine	1,204	1,254	1,261	4.7%	0.6%
Monterey	403,910	421,463	425,356	5.3%	0.9%
Alameda	1,453,136	1,513,859	1,530,620	5.3%	1.1%

Source: California Department of Finance

Some of the growth rates over this past decade have been nothing short of amazing. Despite already having a large population, Riverside County grew by a third over the seven-year period. Several counties had rates in excess of 20%. We do not see growth rates like these being sustained, particularly in the wake of the 2007-2008 credit crisis and the host of other state-wide economic issues we outlined above. But we do see the basic trends remaining intact, driven by prices and cost of living concerns. These trends will be more obvious in the following two illustrations, Figures 15.4 and 15.5.

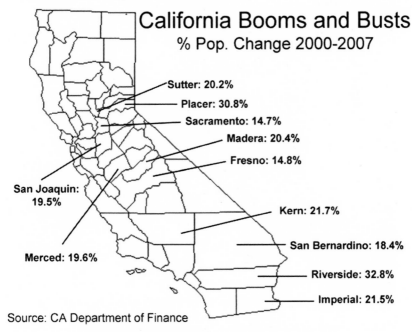

California Booms and Busts
% Pop. Change 2000-2007

Sutter: 20.2%
Placer: 30.8%
Sacramento: 14.7%
Madera: 20.4%
Fresno: 14.8%
San Joaquin: 19.5%
Kern: 21.7%
San Bernardino: 18.4%
Merced: 19.6%
Riverside: 32.8%
Imperial: 21.5%

Source: CA Department of Finance

Figure 15.4 California Population Booms

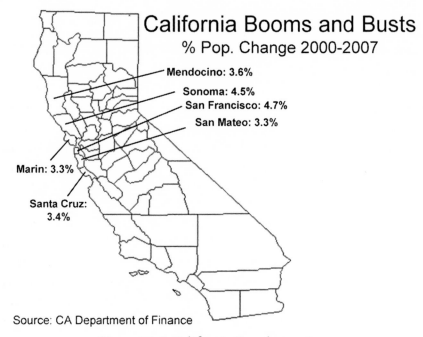

Figure 15.5 California Population Busts

Figures 15.4 and 15.5 illustrate the patterns we described above and in previous chapters. The exurban counties that surround Los Angeles are growing at a torrid pace, while the urban core has grown only modestly. These high-growth counties are Kern, San Bernardino, Riverside, and Imperial. Inland areas of the state centered around Sacramento and Fresno have grown exceptionally fast as well.

Meanwhile, the counties along the coast of Northern California, such as Santa Cruz, San Mateo, San Francisco, Marin, Sonoma, and Mendocino are experiencing lackluster growth at a rate far below the national and state-wide averages. Most of the rest of the state is either sparsely populated or is growing more or less at the state-wide rate.

The reasons for the disparity are due both to economics and public policy. Housing and property taxes are generally cheaper in the high-growth areas, and young families generally prefer a suburban setting with single-family homes and larger yards. School districts are also a factor in many cases. Furthermore, in many of the slow-growing areas, there are also land and property restrictions in place that limit growth and increase costs for existing properties. This is not necessarily a bad thing for property owners and environmental enthusiasts, but it has the effect of pricing newcomers out of the market. It also reduces the potential for growth for local businesses in the area, though again, this is by design.

It also has an effect on local government policy. What will the slow-growing areas do with excess capacity in their schools? Convert them to senior centers? Swings sets to shuffleboard? All joking aside, this has been advocated in certain areas. Meanwhile, the growing areas are struggling to build schools fast enough to meet the demand from new students.

The last years of this decade should prove to be interesting. The fast-growing areas were often those with the largest numbers of young, subprime, and marginal buyers who purchased their homes with exotic mortgages and who are now at the greatest risk of default. So, it is these areas that could suffer the most in the short-term. Over time, the trends should reassert themselves, but homeowners, businesses, and local governments will likely have to suffer through a few lean years in the meantime.

Furthermore, given the demographic trends shaping the economic future of the country at large, some of the hardest-hit areas of the state might not recover at all, or at least not for a decade or more. Plus, continued high taxes and cost of living could accelerate middle-class flight out of California, leaving a state dominated by rich and poor. This is not conducive to economic and social stability.

California has unique issues facing it. The state's prognosis is far more favorable than those of the old Rust Belt states of the Upper Midwest. That said, California's western neighbors all appear to have brighter futures than the Golden State. On balance, we see California more or less following the national trend. There will likely always be opportunities in the state, though the coming years should be quite challenging.

Chapter 16: A Note on the Housing Bust

As of the fourth quarter of 2008, the housing bust continues to cast a pall over the areas most affected. Particularly in the areas where the bubble was most pronounced, there have been plenty of anecdotal stories of people "trapped" in their houses, underwater on their mortgages and unable to sell. When their adjustable rate mortgages were re-set, many of these new homeowners found themselves unable to pay and simply abandoned their homes. This is a nightmare for local mortgage bankers who suddenly find themselves with inventory to sell and no buyers.

These mortgage defaults will eventually cycle through the system, and the houses in question will either find new owners or will have their mortgages renegotiated by the current owners. The incoming Obama Administration might also have plans to renegotiate mortgages from the top down. Regardless, prices could go a lot lower before finally finding a bottom, if Figure 16.1 is any indication.

Home Price-to-Income

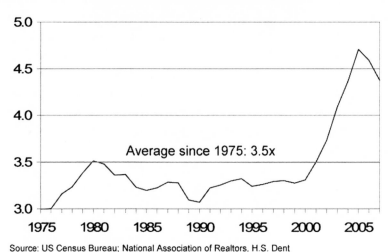

Source: US Census Bureau; National Association of Realtors, H.S. Dent

Figure 16.1: Home Price-to-Income

Despite two years of falling home prices amidst the financing meltdown, prices are still far above past averages, as measured by multiples of income. Figure 16.1 is a "scare chart" that became quite popular at the peak of the bubble. But should this chart be cause for alarm? The median American family income is approximately $50,000. At the historic multiple of 3.5x, this would put the median home price at just over $175,000. At the current multiple, the median home price stands at $220,000. This suggests that home prices could continue to fall, though this would be partially offset by natural increases in average income.

Figure 16.2 tells a very different story, however. When measured in terms of payments, home prices are very much in line with historical norms, though certainly higher than their low point in the late 1990s. In the wake of the 2007-2008 credit crisis, mortgage rates are high, due to newfound risk aversion by lenders and a general state of paralysis in the credit markets. We see both of these trends moderating in the coming years, however. Lenders are not likely to return to the days of reckless abandon for several years or even decades, but once the anxieties of the credit crunch are relieved, credit will begin to flow again. And as we discussed in Chapter 3, mild deflation is more likely to be the norm going forward, not inflation.

As Japan discovered, credit contractions and aging demographics are both deflationary. This implies that mortgage rates, and thus mortgage payments, will be lower soon. Unfortunately, it also suggests that home prices will be lower. And speaking of Japan, Figure 16.3 is a very sobering reminder that, despite all attempts to reflate a real estate bubble that has burst, prices can continue to drift inexorably lower for years after the initial pop.

Home Payment-to-Income

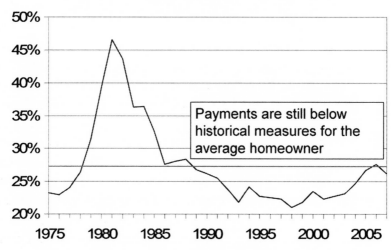

Source: US Census Bureau; National Association of Realtors, Federal Reserve, H.S. Dent

Figure 16.2: Home Payment-to-Income

Japan Residential Condo Price Index: Tokyo 23 Wards

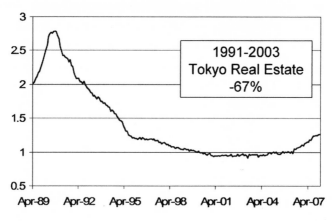

Source: Bloomberg

Figure 16.3: Japan Residential Condo Price Index

So what does all of this mean for U.S. home prices? Do prices "have" to fall as far as they did in Japan? Is another 50% drop likely? It's too early to say at this point. But history and demographic trends suggest that, at least in some geographic areas and some product types, prices could easily fall that much. In virtually all markets, there will likely be a supply glut in upper-middle-class "McMansions," the home of choice for successful middle-aged professionals with children. As we discussed in the opening chapters, the Baby Boomers are already largely past this stage of their lives, and Generation X simply does not have enough people to take their place. Prices may not plummet like they did in Japan, but the plentiful supply combined with the slack in demand virtually guarantees that price increases will be modest at best and that inventory for sale will turnover much more slowly for many years into the future. We would recommend staying away from this segment as an investment class. If you choose to buy one as a primary residence, make sure that you take full advantage of your negotiating power to get the lowest possible price.

The other major area of risk we see is in the speculative condo market. The new supply of luxury, high-end condos in boom areas such as Miami or Sarasota far exceeded even the most optimistic forecasts for demand. In the final stages of the boom, nearly all new demand at the margin was speculative. Condos could be "flipped" multiple times while *still under construction*. If any real estate segments are likely to suffer Japanese-level declines, luxury condos are certainly at the top of the list. Stories abound of entire high-rise towers sitting vacant. Many will eventually be converted into apartments, reversing a multi-year trend in which untold millions of square feet of rental space were converted to condo or time share.

As an anecdotal example, in 2007 it was hard to find a hotel bed in Key West, as so many of the island's properties had been converted and sold, mostly to "investors" who rarely if ever used the properties. We suspect that most of this square footage will revert to apartment and holiday rental space in the coming years as the laws of economics re-exert their control. "Investors," if they haven't already, will discover that condos that earn no income while sitting empty for 50 weeks out of the year while declining precipitously in price make poor investments.

Not all markets reached the speculative madness of South Florida, of course, though there were definite signs of excess in Las Vegas, Phoenix, Washington D.C., Boston, New York City, and much of the state of California. The ability of these real estate markets to recover will depend on their respective demographic and migration trends and on the level of the bubble that preceded the bust. In other words, the areas and product segments that saw the greatest excesses should be the ones that take the longest to recover. These will be the areas most likely to resemble Japan, as illustrated in Figure 16.3.

The greatest opportunities in the coming years should be in apartments and starter homes for the up-and-coming Echo Boomer generation, the children of the Baby Boomers. Apartments and starter homes, if purchased at a reasonable price that allows for positive monthly cash flow, should make fine investments. There might also be money to be made in condo-to-apartment conversions.

The key point here is that time is your friend. In every reasonable scenario, virtually all housing segments have further to fall in the coming years. We would recommend waiting until rental rates firm up, which, given the supply of condos that are likely to be converted, is not likely to be any time in the next several months.

Concluding Remarks

Throughout these pages, we have covered several recurring themes. Global demographics are changing, and with them the world economy. In a world that is becoming ever more interdependent, many of the old rules of thumb need to be reexamined.

For example, the Federal Reserve has been criticized for not raising rates sooner when it became obvious that there was a potentially destructive housing bubble underway in the United States. But how much power did the Fed have to cool the economy when banks and hedge funds could borrow from Japan at 0% for most of the decade? Likewise, the Fed lowered rates in the United States after the "tech wreck" of 2000-2002 with the intention of stimulating the economy. The result was not an upsurge in American production, but rather Chinese production. Greenspan inadvertently fueled the Chinese export boom, which lead the United States to its dangerously high trade deficit, which in turn was one of the factors that caused the dollar to plummet relative to most world currencies.

Today, the Fed is again attempting to stimulate the economy, increasing the money supply to levels that are alarming to many observers. The Fed's actions have thus far failed to be inflationary, as money and credit are being "destroyed" via deleveraging and a decline in the velocity of money faster than the Fed can create it. As a student of Depression economics, Fed Chairman Bernanke knows this, but it doesn't mean that there is much he can do about it.

Meanwhile, the macro trend underlying it all is the aging of America's Baby Boomers. The maturing of the Baby Boomers into early middle age defined the great economic boom of the 1980s and 1990s. In the mid-2000s, the entire world economy benefited from the peak spending years of this mammoth generation.

Unfortunately, we can no longer expect Baby Boomer spending to bail us out. The Boomers have already plateaued in their spending and are now entering their peak savings years. This should put downward pressure on GDP and consumer spending growth for years to come and will significantly contribute to the deflationary forces that will plague the economy.

Meanwhile, the retirement of the Baby Boomers will be the single biggest economic crisis to face the federal, state, and local governments. Social Security will be technically insolvent as early as 2014, when the "trust fund" will be exhausted and the program will have to depend on the government's general revenues. But as serious a crisis as Social Security funding is, it pales in comparison to that of Medicare. Given current assumptions, Medicare would single-handedly bankrupt the United States if benefits were paid in full. Clearly, they won't be. The same goes for the pension and healthcare liabilities that state and local governments owe their current and retired public employees. The resolution to these crises is unpleasant, but there is a strong consensus as to what that resolution is: some combination of higher taxes and fees, lower public services, and a reduction in benefits for the retirees. The negotiations will drag on for years, and they will not be fun to live through.

Finally, the housing bubble and subsequent burst wreaked havoc on the areas most affected. Though California always seems to be in the midst of some budget crisis or another, the one that the state faces today might be the worst in its history. The destruction left in the wake of the housing collapse is largely to blame. It is impossible to know when the housing market will find a bottom and begin to recover. But given the level of inventory still on the market, it could still be several years away. Demographics again play a role here. Demand going forward should be at the lower end of the market in starter homes appropriate for first-time buyers. The "McMansion" market designed for upper-middle-class, middle-aged professionals will likely stagnate for many, many years into the future.

Stock and bond investors face an unusual market going forward. Growth prospects look bleak, but at the same time stock valuations have been pushed down to levels not seen in multiple decades and non-government bond prices now offer a rich risk premium. Still, in this market, a buy-and-hold strategy is inappropriate. Nearly twenty years after its bubble peak, the Japanese Nikkei stock index is down more than

75%. We recommend that investors construct a portfolio appropriate for their risk profile, rebalance that portfolio regularly to "buy low and sell high" and in particular, pay attention to the fundamentals that really drive an economy—you.

With crisis comes opportunity. And though we recommend prudence and caution, we are enthusiastic about the prospects for profiting from a changing consumer economy in the years to come.

Appendix

Growth vs. Value

	Russell 1000 Growth	Russell 1000 Value	Russell 2000 Growth	Russell 2000 Value
1979	23.88	20.52	50.85	35.37
1980	39.56	24.41	52.26	25.38
1981	(11.32)	1.24	(9.24)	14.86
1982	20.45	20.05	20.97	28.52
1983	15.98	28.30	20.13	38.65
1984	(0.95)	10.10	(15.84)	2.27
1985	32.86	31.52	30.95	31.00
1986	15.37	19.97	3.58	7.41
1987	5.30	0.50	(10.48)	(7.11)
1988	11.27	23.17	20.37	29.47
1989	35.94	25.21	20.17	12.43
1990	(0.26)	(8.09)	(17.42)	(21.78)
1991	41.27	24.56	51.19	41.72
1992	4.99	13.59	7.77	29.14
1993	2.87	18.07	13.36	23.79
1994	2.64	(1.98)	(2.42)	(1.53)
1995	37.19	38.34	31.04	25.74
1996	23.12	21.65	11.26	21.37
1997	30.48	35.18	12.94	31.80
1998	38.70	15.64	1.23	(6.43)
1999	33.16	7.35	43.10	(1.49)
2000	(22.43)	7.02	(22.44)	22.80
2001	(20.42)	(5.59)	(9.23)	14.02
2002	(27.89)	(15.52)	(30.27)	(11.42)
2003	29.76	30.03	48.53	46.02

2004			
2005	5.27	7.04	4.15	4.70
2006	9.09	22.21	13.35	23.48
2007	11.81	(0.18)	7.05	(9.76)
2008	(38.44)	(36.85)	(38.54)	(28.93)
Annual Return	11.85	13.13	10.76	14.79
Standard Deviation	21.19	16.37	24.22	19.23

(2004 row: 6.30 | 16.49 | 14.31 | 22.25)

Correlation Between Asset Classes

	Russell 1000 Growth	Russell 1000 Value	Russell 2000 Growth	Russell 2000 Value
Russell 1000 Growth	1	0.81	0.84	0.49
Russell 1000 Value	0.81	1.00	0.76	0.82
Russell 2000 Growth	0.84	0.76	1.00	0.71
Russell 2000 Value	0.49	0.82	0.71	1.00

Source: Bloomberg, Steele Systems (orginal data by Morningstar)

Russell 1000 Growth Index measures the performance of those Russell 1000 companies with higher price-to-book ratios and higher forecasted growth values.

Russell 1000 Value Index measures the performance of those Russell 1000 companies with lower price-to-book ratios and lower forecasted growth values.

Russell 2000 Growth Index measures the performance of those Russell 2000 companies with higher price-to-book ratios and higher forcasted growth values.

Russell 2000 Value Index measures the performance of those Russell 2000 companies with lower price-to-book ratios and lower forcasted growth values.

U.S. vs. International

	Fixed Income	US Large Companies	US Small Companies	Int'l Large Companies	Int'l Small Companies
1973	3.40	(14.70)	(40.70)	(14.20)	(13.70)
1974	7.00	(26.50)	(29.30)	(22.20)	(28.60)
1975	8.30	37.20	69.90	37.10	49.90
1976	11.70	23.90	54.50	3.70	11.50
1977	3.00	(7.20)	22.10	19.40	74.10
1978	2.20	6.60	21.80	34.30	65.50
1979	6.60	18.60	43.10	6.20	(0.80)
1980	6.70	32.50	38.60	24.40	35.50
1981	10.80	(4.90)	2.00	(1.00)	(4.70)
1982	25.40	21.60	25.00	(0.90)	0.80
1983	8.20	22.60	29.10	24.60	32.40
1984	14.30	6.30	(7.30)	7.90	10.10
1985	18.00	31.70	31.10	56.70	60.10
1986	13.10	18.70	5.70	69.90	50.10
1987	3.60	5.30	(8.80)	24.90	70.60
1988	6.40	16.60	25.00	28.60	26.00
1989	12.70	31.60	16.30	10.80	29.30
1990	9.60	(3.10)	(19.50)	(23.20)	(16.80)
1991	14.10	30.40	46.00	12.50	7.10
1992	7.50	7.60	18.40	(11.90)	(18.40)
1993	8.70	10.10	18.90	33.00	33.50
1994	(2.80)	1.30	(1.80)	8.10	12.40
1995	16.40	37.50	28.50	11.60	0.50

Year	Fixed Income	US Large	US Small	Int'l Large	Int'l Small
1996	3.40	23.00	16.50	6.40	2.60
1997	8.00	33.40	22.40	2.10	(24.60)
1998	9.10	28.60	(2.60)	20.30	5.40
1999	(0.10)	21.00	21.30	27.30	17.70
2000	10.70	(9.10)	(3.00)	(14.00)	(9.20)
2001	8.60	(11.90)	2.50	(21.20)	(14.30)
2002	11.00	(22.10)	(20.50)	(15.70)	(9.60)
2003	2.40	28.70	47.30	39.30	57.80
2004	2.10	10.80	18.40	20.70	28.10
2005	0.71	4.91	4.62	10.89	23.89
2006	3.53	15.79	18.44	23.47	17.35
2007	9.87	5.49	(1.56)	8.63	(0.35)
2008	12.2	(37.00)	(33.79)	(43.09)	(48.36)
Annual Return	8.2	11.0	13.3	11.5	15.5
Growth of $10,000	$164,756	$241,135	$356,361	$225,401	$513,075
Standard Deviation	5.6	18.9	24.8	23.2	30.0
Worst 1 year	(2.8) 1994	-37.0 2008	(40.7) 2008	(43.09) 2008	(48.36) 2008
Worst 3 year	5.1 2002-04	(37.6) 2000-02	(28.8) 1973-75	(42.9) 2000-02	(40.8) 2000-02
Worst 5 year	31.2 2004-08	(11.0) 2000-04	(6.6) 1998-02	(12.5) 1998-02	(12.7) 1998-02

Fixed Income - Lehman Govt Corp/TR 1973-1991, Bloomberg 3-5 year Gov't Bond 1992-2008
US Large - S&P 500 1973-2008
US Small - DFA US Small Company 1973-1978, Russell 2000 Small Company 1979-2008
Int'l Large - MSCI EAFE 1973-2008
Int'l Small - DFA Int'l Small Company 1973-1996, MSCI EAFE Small 1997-2008

Asset Allocation Models

	Fixed Income	(Capital Preservation) 20% Equity	(Balanced Income) 40% Equity	(Balanced) 60% Equity	(Balanced Growth) 75% Equity	(Growth) 90% Equity	(Aggressive) 100% Equity	S&P 500 Index
1973	3.4	(2.0)	(7.4)	(13.1)	(17.1)	(21.1)	(23.6)	(14.7)
1974	7.0	0.2	(6.6)	(13.5)	(18.5)	(23.7)	(27.0)	(26.5)
1975	8.3	16.6	24.9	33.6	39.8	45.9	49.9	37.2
1976	11.7	15.4	19.2	23.4	25.7	28.7	30.3	23.9
1977	3.0	5.4	7.9	10.3	13.0	14.0	15.2	(7.2)
1978	2.2	6.2	10.1	13.9	17.6	19.9	22.0	6.6
1979	6.6	10.0	13.3	17.0	19.2	21.9	23.4	18.6
1980	6.7	12.1	17.5	23.1	27.0	31.1	33.7	32.5
1981	10.8	8.3	5.7	3.2	1.4	(0.6)	(1.9)	(4.9)
1982	25.4	23.8	22.2	20.8	19.1	18.3	17.3	21.6
1983	8.2	11.8	15.4	19.0	21.8	24.4	26.2	22.6
1984	14.3	11.9	9.4	6.9	5.1	3.3	2.2	6.3
1985	18.0	22.0	26.0	29.8	33.4	35.9	38.1	31.7
1986	13.1	15.5	17.8	19.6	22.4	23.5	25.0	18.7
1987	3.6	4.8	6.1	7.0	8.6	9.0	9.8	5.3
1988	6.4	9.6	12.8	15.9	18.5	20.7	22.3	16.6
1989	12.7	14.7	16.8	18.9	20.1	21.9	22.9	31.6
1990	9.6	5.0	0.5	(4.1)	(7.9)	(10.9)	(13.2)	(3.1)
1991	14.1	17.4	20.8	24.5	26.5	29.3	30.8	30.4
1992	7.5	7.2	6.8	6.8	6.1	6.2	5.9	7.6

	A	B	C	D	E	F	G	H
1993	8.7	10.8	12.8	14.7	16.7	17.9	19.0	10.1
1994	(2.8)	(1.8)	(0.7)	0.2	1.1	1.8	2.3	1.3
1995	16.4	18.5	20.5	22.8	23.7	25.8	26.8	37.5
1996	3.4	6.0	8.5	11.2	12.7	15.0	16.2	23.0
1997	8.0	10.2	12.4	14.8	15.7	18.1	19.1	33.4
1998	9.1	10.1	11.1	11.9	12.4	13.5	14.1	28.6
1999	(0.1)	4.3	8.6	12.9	16.3	19.5	21.7	21.0
2000	10.7	7.0	3.3	(0.2)	(3.1)	(5.8)	(7.7)	(9.1)
2001	8.6	5.2	1.8	(1.4)	(4.2)	(6.7)	(8.5)	(11.9)
2002	11.0	4.9	(1.1)	(7.2)	(11.6)	(16.3)	(19.3)	(22.1)
2003	2.4	9.9	17.3	24.9	30.7	36.0	39.7	28.7
2004	2.1	5.0	7.9	10.8	13.2	15.2	16.7	10.8
2005	0.7	2.1	3.5	4.8	6.0	6.9	7.6	4.9
2006	3.5	6.4	9.3	12.2	14.5	16.6	18.0	15.8
2007	9.9	8.6	7.4	6.0	5.1	4.1	3.6	5.5
2008	12.2	2.2	(7.8)	(17.8)	(25.5)	(32.9)	(37.9)	(37.0)
Annual Return	8.2	9.1	9.9	10.7	11.3	11.9	12.3	11.0
Growth of $10,000	$164,756	$214,327	$264,625	$310,805	$339,271	$351,654	$354,442	$241,135
Standard Deviation	5.6	6.1	8.7	12.2	15.0	17.8	19.7	18.9
Worst 1 year	(2.8) 1994	(2.0) 1973	(7.8) 2008	(17.8) 2008	(25.5) 2008	(32.9) 2008	(37.9) 2008	(37.0) 2008
Worst 3 year	5.1 2000-02	14.5 1973-75	4.0 2000-2	(8.8) 2000-2	(18.0) 2000-2	(26.4) 2000-2	(31.9) 2000-2	(37.6) 2000-2

195

See important disclosure information. Past performance cannot guarantee comparable future results.

The results reflected in the presentation materials are hypothetical results that were achieved by means of the retroactive application of a hypothetical example, and, as such, the corresponding results have inherent limitations, including: (1) the hypothetical results do not reflect the results of actual trading using client assets, but were achieved by means of the retroactive application of a hypothetical example that was designed with the benefit of hindsight; (2) the hypothetical results do not the deduction of transaction, custodial or advisory fees, the deduction of which would have the effect of decreasing model performance results; (3) performance may not reflect the impact that any material market or economic factors might have had on the adviser's use of the hypothetical if the hypothetical had been used during the period to actually mange client assets; and, (4) RCM clients may have experienced investment results during the corresponding time periods that were materially different from those portrayed in the hypothetical. Past performance may not be indicative of future results. Therefore, no current or prospective client should assume that future performance will be profitable, will equal the reflected historic hypothetical performance results or the performance results for any of the comparative index benchmarks provided. The historical index performance results are provided exclusively for comparison purposes only. It should not be assumed that account holdings will correspond directly to any of the comparative index benchmarks. To the extent that there has been a change in a client's investment objectives or financial situation, he/she/it is encouraged to advise RCM immediately. Different types of investments and/or investment strategies involve varying levels of risk, and there can be no assurance that any specific investment or investment strategy (including the investments purchased and/or investment strategies devised by RCM) will be either suitable or profitable for a client's or prospective client's portfolio. Unless otherwise noted on the presentation page (see Data Sources below), all hypothetical results have been compiled solely by RCM, are unaudited, and have not been independently verified. Information pertaining to RCM's advisory operations, services, and fees is set forth in RCM's current written disclosure statement, a copy of which is available from RCM upon request. No presentation participant should assume that any such discussion serves as the receipt of, or a substitute for, personalized advice from RCM or from any other investment professional. RCM is neither an attorney nor an accountant, and no portion of this content should be interpreted as legal, accounting or tax advice.

Data Source: The following data source was used to develop the tables and figures in this material. Note that many of our return series rely on data and market history provided by Bloomberg Professional. All performance data are total returns including interest and dividends.

See important disclosure information. Past performance cannot guarantee comparable future results.

Model Portfolios and Market Indexes

• Yearly rebalancing.

• Equity Indexes:
US Large Companies – S&P500 Index 1973-2008
US Small Companies – DFA US Small Co. 1973-1978, Russell 2000 (Small Co.) 1979-2008
Intl Large Companies – MSCI EAFE Index 1973-2008
Intl Small Companies – DFA US Small Co. 1973-1996 (DFA simulation back to 1970)
MSCI EAFE Small Cap 1997-2008
• Fixed Income Index:
Lehman Government Corporate Total Return 1973-1991
Bloomberg Government 3-5 year Total Return 1992-2008

Model Portfolios - Strategic (buy and hold) Asset Allocation

Fixed Income: 100% Fixed Income

Capital Preservation: 80% Fixed Income, 8% US Large Companies, 7% US Small Companies, 3% Intl Large Companies, 2% Intl Small Companies
Balanced Income: 60% Fixed Income, 16% US Large Companies, 14% US Small Companies, 6% Intl Large Companies, 4% Intl Small Companies
Balanced: 40% Fixed Income, 24% US Large Companies, 22% US Small Companies, 8% Intl Large Companies, 6% Intl Small Companies
Balanced Growth: 25% Fixed Income, 28% US Large Companies, 27% US Small Companies, 12% Intl Large Companies, 8% Intl Small Companies
Growth: 10% Fixed Income, 36% US Large Companies, 32% US Small Companies, 13% Intl Large Companies, 9% Intl Small Companies
Aggressive Growth: 40% US Large Companies, 35% US Small Companies, 15% Intl Large Companies, 10% Intl Small Companies

Index

Free Periodic E-Mail Updates

Would you like to receive free periodic updates from the authors of Boom or Bust? If you enjoyed the book and would like to get additional commentary from Douglas Robinson and Charles Sizemore, please visit:

http://www.boombust.org/

Complete the online form, and you will be added to Robinson and Sizemore's e-mail distribution list. From time to time, Robinson and Sizemore will send updates covering the themes discussed in this book.

This service is absolutely free, and your personal information will remain confidential. We will not share your e-mail address with third-party marketers or spammers.

Printed in the United States
145797LV00003B/215/P

9 780595 510030